Digital Imaging

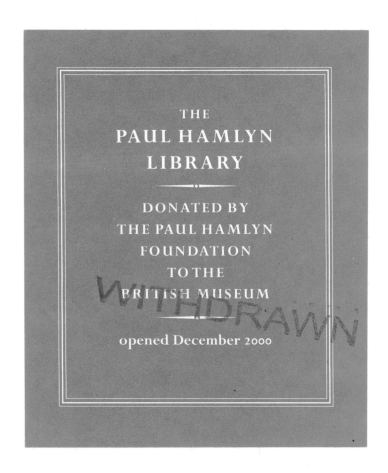

ABOUT THE SERIES

The American Association for State and Local History Book Series publishes technical and professional information for those who practice and support history, and addresses issues critical to the field of state and local history. To submit a proposal or manuscript to the series, please request proposal guidelines from AASLH headquarters: AASLH Book Series, 1717 Church St., Nashville, Tennessee 37203. Telephone: (615) 320-3203. Fax: (615) 327-9013. Website: www.aaslh.org.

ABOUT THE ORGANIZATION

The American Association for State and Local History (AASLH) is a nonprofit educational organization dedicated to advancing knowledge, understanding, and appreciation of local history in the United States and Canada. In addition to sponsorship of this book series, the Association publishes the periodical *History News*, a newsletter, technical leaflets and reports, and other materials; confers prizes and awards in recognition of outstanding achievement in the field; and supports a broad education program and other activities designed to help members work more effectively. To join the organization, contact: Membership Director, AASLH, 1717 Church St., Nashville, Tennessee 37203.

Digital Imaging

A Practical Approach

JILL MARIE KOELLING

ALTAMIRA
PRESS

A Division of
ROWMAN & LITTLEFIELD PUBLISHERS, INC.
Walnut Creek • Lanham • New York • Toronto • Oxford

For my family

AltaMira Press
A Division of Rowman & Littlefield Publishers, Inc.
1630 North Main Street, #367
Walnut Creek, CA 94596
www.altamirapress.com

Rowman & Littlefield Publishers, Inc.
A wholly owned subsidary of The Rowman & Littlefield Publishing Group, Inc.
4501 Forbes Boulevard, Suite 200
Lanham, MD 20706

PO Box 317
Oxford
OX2 9RU, UK

British Library Cataloguing in Publication Information Available

Library of Congress Cataloging-in-Publication Data

Koelling, Jill Marie, 1966–
  Digital imaging : a practical approach / Jill Marie Koelling.
      p.   cm.—(American Association for State and Local History book series)
    Includes bibliographical references and index.
    ISBN 0-7591-0445-X (alk. paper)—ISBN 0-7591-0446-8 (pbk. : alk. paper)
    1. Digital preservation.   2. Library materials—Digitization.   3. Archival materials—
  Digitization.   I. Title.   II. Series.

  Z681.3.D53.K64   2004
  025.8'4—dc22   2003017773

Printed in the United States of America

♾™The paper used in this publication meets the minimum requirements of American National Standard for Information Sciences—Permanence of Paper for Printed Library Materials, ANSI/NISO Z39.48–1992.

Contents

Collection managers, curators, museum directors, archivists, exhibit designers, registrars, and volunteers all face the same problems when it comes to digital imaging. No matter the size of the project, the number of staff available to help, paid or not, digital imaging can be tricky yet a whole lot of fun. Digital imaging is a valuable tool for the dissemination of information held by historical artifacts. This book is designed to help you understand what digital imaging is all about. I've pulled together information from many sources, including my experience the past six years working on digital projects at the Nebraska State Historical Society.

Rather unconventionally, I start in chapter 1 with a glossary. It is very important to speak "digital." So instead of putting the glossary in the back, I want you to read it first. It is more than just a list of terms. I also include some discussion about a few important issues, like watermarks and image compression. These topics are covered later, but start first with the glossary. Get comfortable with the language so that the rest of the book will be easy to understand.

The meat of the book comes in chapters 5 through 7 where I give specifics on what to look for when buying a scanner (although I do not recommend specific manufacturers), describe how to establish image file benchmarks and achieve your goals, and explain what metadata is exactly and why it is important. I've also included lists of questions to ask and answer before starting a digital project, guidelines for staffing needs and duties, and plenty of illustrations to help explain what all this means.

Just for fun and because not much is being said about the unexpected benefits of digital projects, I've included chapter 8 on image manipulation and how it can enhance historical research and how using digital technology can recover information from severely deteriorated originals.

I've tried to include examples of digitizing all types of objects. Many institutions as well as a majority of the written resources available on digital imaging focus first and foremost on photographs; however, literally everything can now be digitized.

The first digital project undertaken by the Nebraska State Historical Society was the digitization of Solomon D. Butcher photographs and the Uriah Oblinger family collection. We chose these two collections because together they tell the story of homesteading on the Great Plains. The project was funded through a 1997–1998 award from the Library of Congress/Ameritech Digital Library competition. All together, more than three thousand glass plate negatives, a few dozen 1920s-era prints, several cased portraits (including a few ambrotypes and tintypes), as well as over six thousand pages of manuscript material were digitized and are now part of the American Memory portion of the Library of Congress website. The digitization process took two years to complete. We had a staff of twelve, mostly grant-funded temporary employees, not including the dozen or so volunteers who came and went as the project progressed. Not only did we digitize the collections, but we also item-level cataloged each image and letter, created an online family tree and genealogy of the Oblingers, and generated SGML-tagged text documents for each letter, in order to make them word-searchable. (*SGML* stands for standard generalized markup language.) SGML tags, similar to HTML (hypertext markup language) tags, are used to define how a document is displayed or formatted. SGML tags are particularly useful when dealing with historical documents because they offer a standardized structure for a variety of computer programs to interpret and display.[1]

Since completing the American Memory project, the Nebraska State Historical Society has digitized more than twenty-five thousand items from its collections, including photographs, manuscripts, archeological materials, and museum objects.

ACKNOWLEDGMENTS

This publication could not have been possible without the generous support and encouragement of the staff of the Nebraska State Historical Society (NSHS), in particular the director, Lawrence Sommer, without whose backing the digital imaging efforts at the society would not have been possible. I must say a special thank you to my former colleagues of the library archives division at the NSHS, who put up with my technobabble and constant requests for new digitization equipment for nearly eight years. Thank you, John Carter, for believing in digital technology and how it changes the world of photographic research. Thank you, Paul Eisloeffel, for giving up your assistant so that she could pursue the digital world. I would like to thank the staff of the NSHS conservation division as well, particularly Julie Reilly, for embracing digital technology with open arms and seeing a future for a partnership between conservation and digitization. I also want to thank Terry Davis, president and CEO, and Harry Klinkhamer, program officer, at the American Association for State and Local History. Their efforts to help spread the word about proper digitization techniques are a direct reflection of their insightful leadership. Thanks must also go out to Susan Walters at AltaMira Press, for helping make this book become a reality. Her guidance made my life easier. I want to say thank you as well to Lynne Ireland. From our first meeting over ten years ago, you have been a constant voice of support and encouragement in my life. Thank you to my fellow scanning technicians at the NSHS. I could not have accomplished any of this without you. And finally, thank you to all my friends who let me talk nonstop about digital technology and how it shapes our world. You are all terrific listeners and I appreciate each and every one of you.

NOTE

1. For complete information, especially a detailed discussion of the digitization process, check out this link: http://memory.loc.gov/ammem/award98/nbhihtml/build.html. To access the results of this project online, go to http://memory.loc.gov/ammem/award98/nbhihtml/pshome.html.

CHAPTER 1

A Digital Glossary

SO WHAT IS A JPEG, AND WHAT IS IMPORTANT TO KNOW about it? As with any new technology, digital imaging comes with its own language. Before beginning a digital project, it is important to have a clear understanding of what that language is and how it will affect your decision making. There are many new terms to know and understand, and this chapter is designed to help you reach that goal.

The terms in the glossary are organized in alphabetical order to make it easier to go back to a term as needed. Reading a glossary may not sound exciting; however, the terms listed here are used repeatedly throughout this work. If you decide not to take the time to read this first, be sure to look back at the glossary as you make your way through the rest of the text if you run across language you do not understand. Boldface words within a definition are also listed in the glossary.

ARTIFACTS (NOISE)

The term *artifact* is used to describe squiggles or jumbled parts of an image file. They are usually introduced through extreme image manipulation, **lossy compression**, or the use of sharpening features in the scanning software.

BATCH PROCESSING

Batch processing is a tool available in some **image manipulation software** packages that allows the user to program the software to run a series of events automatically on a particular set of image files. For example, the software is programmed to open the master files in a particular folder, change the **resolution** and **pixel dimension**, or save the newly manipulated files in a separate folder, leaving the masters intact, and close the newly created files. Running batch programs increases productivity. The software can open, perform the events, and save and close the files much more quickly than a person using a mouse or keyboard for the same actions.

BENCHMARKS

An established set of criteria, including **spatial resolution**, **optical resolution**, **bit depth**, and **file format**, used to create your image files. (For more information on establishing benchmarks, see chapter 5, "Technical Specifications.")

BETA TESTING

Running a series of tests on a website before it goes live for public use. This gives your institution time to find any problems and fix them before the public has access to your site.

BIT DEPTH

A *bit* is the smallest piece of information in an image file. A pixel is capable of displaying multiple bits. Many scanners will capture in forty-eight bits, meaning more color or shades of gray are recorded from the original; however, most image manipulation software does not allow much work with these higher bit depths. The higher the bit depth, the more color information is captured.

Grayscale Capture
8 bit = 256 shades of gray
16 bit = 65,536 shades of gray

Color Capture (RGB)
24 bit = 16 million colors
48 bit = over 281 trillion colors

CCD (CHARGED-COUPLED DEVICE)

The CCD is the capture tool in scanners and digital cameras. Think of it as film. It takes the picture and transforms it into the pixels of a **digital image** file.

CDR/CDRW

CDR or *CD-ROM* stands for compact disk–read only memory. *CDRW* stands for compact disk rewriteable.

Both are used for storage of image files. Many manufactures hype the longevity of their CDRs and CDRWs. Do not be concerned with buying a CD that is advertised to last one hundred years. No computer with a working CD drive will still exist in one hundred years, so even if your institution still has CDs, the staff will have no way of retrieving data from those CDs. (See **refreshment**.) If you decide to use CDRs for image storage, create two sets of CDs and store one set off-site as a backup copy.

DATA

Data is information. The word *data* is now generally used as both singular and plural.

DIGITAL CAMERA

A digital camera is just like a regular camera, except it uses a **CCD** to capture the picture instead of film. Digital cameras range in price from under $100 to over $25,000. The cost difference is directly associated with the size of the CCD chip. The larger the CCD chip, the more information it can capture and the more expensive the camera. This size/dollar comparison is the same with traditional film cameras. The larger the film used in the camera (e.g., 4 × 5 view cameras), the more expensive the camera.

DIGITAL IMAGE

A *digital image* is a computer file generated by a **scanner** or **digital camera**. It is an electronic graphic representation of the object scanned or photographed with the digital camera. The digital image is made up of **pixels**, which are often referred to as **dots**.

DOTS

A dot is also called a **pixel**. For more information, go to the term *pixel* in this glossary.

DPI OR PPI

Dots per inch (*dpi*) and *pixels per inch* (*ppi*) refer to the same thing: the resolution of the image file or the number of pixels in every inch of the image file; for example, 800 ppi means there are eight hundred pixels in every inch of the image file.

DVD

Digital versatile disc. DVDs look like CDRs or CDRWs; however, they can store up to 4.7 gigabytes of data. There are several types of DVDs: DVD+R, DVD–R, DVD±R, and DVDRW. Not all DVD burners use the same type of DVD.

DYNAMIC RANGE

Dynamic range is the number of colors or tones represented in an object. The dynamic range for a **scanner** determines the number of shades of gray or color it can record. The larger the dynamic range, the more shades or colors will be captured.

ELEMENT

The word *element* is used to describe a specific type of data; for example, a *date element* is the date the digital image file was created, and a *subject element* describes the subject of the image file. Elements are often called *fields* in database programs.

FILE FORMAT

File format refers to types of image files. Typical file formats for digital imaging include **TIFF**, **JPEG**, and **GIF**.

GIF (GRAPHIC IMAGE FILE)

GIF image files are strictly black-and-white images. There are no shades of gray in a GIF file, which makes this file format appropriate for line art but not recommended for photographs or other original objects for which capturing shades of gray or color is necessary. This file format is used almost exclusively for image files of published text. The file extension is gif.

IMAGE MANIPULATION SOFTWARE

Software designed to alter image files, for example, adjusting contrast, cropping, rotating, and color correction. The list of image manipulation software packages is long and varied, beginning with the most popular Adobe Photoshop® and Adobe Photoshop Elements and including Corel Draw Essentials, Ulead PhotoImpact, Microsoft Digital Imaging Pro, Jasc Paint Shop, and software packages available for download from the Internet such as the Gimp (GNU Image Manipulation Program) and ImageMagick.

IMAGE PROCESSING

Making additional copies of the master files, called *surrogate files*, for use on the Internet, for making prints, or for any other needs. This may also include some image manipulation to the surrogate files.

JPEG (JOINT PHOTOGRAPHIC EXPERT GROUP)

A *JPEG* is a compressed image file format, which means the file is shrunk and data is adjusted to make the file size smaller and therefore faster to transmit over the Internet and less bulky for storage. It is the preferred file format for digital image files posted on the Internet. The file extension is jpg, with the *e* in *JPEG* dropped for the extension. Caution: Information may be lost due to the compression that occurs when creating a jpeg file. See **lossless versus lossy compression**.

A risk of long-term retrievability of the file itself is associated with using the JPEG file format for master files. Once a file is compressed, software is required to decompress the file properly in order to open it. As file formats change and software changes, it is risky to maintain master image files as compressed files. At some point, the file compression will require software no longer available, making the master files irretrievable.

LOSSLESS VERSUS LOSSY COMPRESSION

In general, compressing a file reduces the file's storage space requirements. Lossy compression occurs when an image file is compressed to the point that it loses data. In lossy compression, data is lost because the software takes an average of a series of pixels and makes them all the same value. Then when the file is uncompressed for viewing, all of the pixels in that series become the same value.

Lossless compression allows an image file to be compressed without losing data. In lossless compression, the software records all the data from each pixel in the series but in such a way that it retains all the information. When the file is uncompressed for viewing, all of the pixels are displayed with their original values.

Figure 1.1 shows what happens to information during lossless versus lossy compression. Compare the sets of ones and zeros before and after compression, and notice the difference in the sets under lossy compression. The one and zero combinations are no longer identical to the

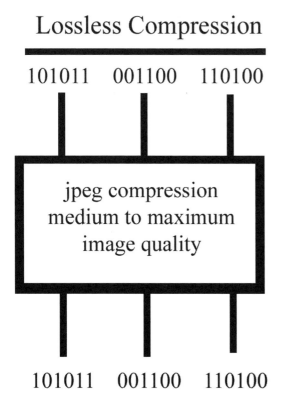

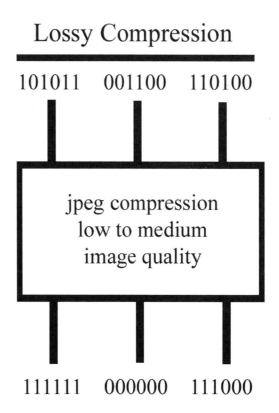

Figure 1.1 Lossy versus Lossless Compression.

original set, distorting the image file. This distortion is often referred to as **artifacts** or **noise**. Examine the close-up section of the photograph shown in figure 1.2 to see the artifacts created by lossy compression (figure 1.4). It makes the photograph look fuzzy. In reality, the lossy compression has eliminated information from the image file. Lossy compression exists because the software program that creates the compression is capable of extreme compression. Some situations that do not require all information be retained utilize lossy compression to create extremely small file sizes. Digital imaging requires no loss of data or lossless compression (see figure 1.3).

MASTER IMAGE FILE

The *master image file* is the original computer file generated by the scanner or digital camera.

MEDIA

For the purposes of this book, *media* is the material used to store data. The word *media* is now often used as both singular or plural. Types of media include but are not limited to **CD-ROMs**, **DVDs**, floppy disks, and hard drives.

METADATA

Metadata is, literally, data about data. It is information about information. For the purposes of digital imaging, *metadata* is information recorded about the creation of the digital image. It may also include information about the original object as well. (For more information on metadata, see chapter 7.)

OPTICAL RESOLUTION

Optical resolution is the maximum number of **pixels** the **scanner** can record without interpolating or guessing information. Optical resolution is true information. It is dependent on the sophistication of the scanner. High-end **scanners** will have optical resolutions in the range of 2,000 ppi. Low-end scanners will be closer to 600 ppi.

PIXELS (DOTS)

A *pixel* is the part of the digital image file that contains the image of the object. The pixel can display many dif-

ferent shades of gray or many different colors. Pixels are little pieces of information that when put together make an image file.

Pixels are often called *dots*, as in **dots per inch** (**dpi**), rather than **pixels per inch** (**ppi**). The use of the word *dot* rather than *pixel* was adopted to help people understand what pixels really are. *Dot* is a term pulled from the print world, where dots make up the image in a published photograph. Look at any photograph in a book or newspaper with a magnifying glass, and you will see dots. Pixels are to digital image files what dots are to published photographs.

PIXEL DIMENSIONS

The number of pixels in a digital image file. For example: 640 pixels wide by 480 pixels high. (See **spatial resolution**.)

QUALITY CONTROL

Quality control is the act of comparing an image file to your established benchmarks. It is vital to carry out quality control on all image files, but most importantly master files.

RGB

Red, green, blue. RGB is the setting most scanners and digital cameras use to capture color image files. The **CCD** itself is designed to interpret only red, green, and blue. Every color image file created is a mixture of red, green, and blue. Think of a painter's palette and mixing paint colors to create new ones. In a sense that is what happens when an image file is created.

REFERENCE FILE

A *reference file* is a **surrogate image**, generated from the master file for use on a web page. The reference file is the primary file used by visitors on a website. Reference files are usually less than 150 ppi and no more than 640 pixels on their long dimension; however, some reference files can be as high as 300 ppi and 3,000 pixels long.

REFRESHMENT

Refreshment is the transfer of digital image files, or any computer file, from one media to another in order to

Figure 1.2   Nebraska State Historical Society (NSHS) RG5251.PH-4.

Figure 1.3   Close-up of NSHS RG5251.PH-4: Lossless Compression = No Loss of Information.

Figure 1.4   Close-up of NSHS RG5251.PH-4: Lossy Compression = Considerable Loss of Information. Notice the "artifacts."

ensure continued access to those files. This is the most important aspect of digital image projects and one frequently overlooked.

Computer technology changes so quickly that it is important to ensure that the image files you generate during your digital imaging project can still be retrieved from their storage media in the future. Ask yourself this question: Do you have files on five and a quarter-inch floppy disks and no computer with a five and a quarter-inch floppy drive? Digital imaging is expensive, and you do not want to invest time and energy creating files that you cannot retrieve in five years. Therefore, as technology and storage media change, it is important to transfer your image files from their current media to new media, whatever that may be—DVD or some other form of storage yet to be invented. Refreshment cycles should happen regularly, at least every five years.

Along with refreshment comes the need to check your data. Do not be satisfied with the simple transfer of files. Check to make sure the entire file transferred and that it opens properly. This can be handled through **batch processing** in image manipulation programs.

RESOLUTION

Resolution normally refers to the number of **pixels** in every inch of the image file—for example, 800 pixels per inch. (See **spatial resolution**.)

SCANNER

A *scanner* is the tool used to create digital image files from original materials, such as photographs, negatives, letters, newspapers, and all types of flat media. Scanners contain a **CCD**, light source, and software that combine to create a **digital image** file.

SPATIAL RESOLUTION

Spatial resolution refers to the number of **pixels** in an image file (e.g., 1,040 × 1,280 pixels). Resolution is also described as either **dpi**, dots per inch, or **ppi**, pixels per inch. For example, 300 ppi means there are 300 pixels in every inch of the image file. The more pixels per inch, the more information in the image file. For example, an 800 ppi file will contain more information than a 300 ppi file.

SURROGATE IMAGE

Any file generated from the master image file—for example, a **reference file** with a resolution of 150 ppi and a pixel dimension of 640 pixels wide for use on a web page.

TIFF (TAGGED IMAGE FILE FORMAT)

TIFF files are the recommended file format for master image files. TIFF files are uncompressed and can be opened using both the Mac and PC operating systems. The file extension is tif (the second *f* is dropped).

UNINTERPOLATED VERSUS INTERPOLATED

Uninterpolated information is information captured directly by the scanner. Interpolated information is created by the scanner software. Scanning an object at higher than the scanner's **optical resolution** creates image files that have interpolated data added by the software rather than captured from the original, creating inaccuracy.

WATERMARK

Two types of watermarks are currently in use for image files: visible and electronic, sometimes called *digital*, watermarks. Watermarks are used to prove ownership of the image file.

Visible watermarks are a secondary image placed on top of the original image file in an image manipulation program. These watermarks are often placed in areas of the image file that make them difficult to remove. (See figure 1.5.) Alternately, they can be placed in a less critical position. (See figure 1.6.)

Electronic or digital watermarks are invisible and are embedded in the file itself. A *digital watermark* is a code assigned by the watermarking company that is specific to your institution. It does not make the file unprintable or protect the file from unauthorized copying. It does, however, identify the file as the property of your institution. (See figure 1.7.)

Figure 1.5   NSHS RG2608.PH-1048. The NSHS logo was used as a visible watermark in the middle of the image file on the right to make it difficult to remove.

Figure 1.6   NSHS RG2608.PH-1048. In this image, "Copyright 2003, Nebraska State Historical Society, all rights reserved," was added in an area that does not significantly detract from the image itself. It identifies the image as property of the Nebraska State Historical Society and states the file is copyrighted and therefore may not be duplicated without permission. However, two clicks of the mouse in any image manipulation software and the top portion of the image file could be deleted and the copyright statement obliterated.

Figure 1.7   NSHS RG2608.PH-1048. This image file has an embedded digital watermark that is undetectable except by software packages that look for watermarks.

CHAPTER 2

Questions to Ask before Starting a Digital Project

ACCESS VERSUS PRESERVATION IS AN AGE-OLD PROBLEM in the museum and archive profession. Do we hide the collection in order to preserve it, or do we offer access in order to enrich our knowledge of the past? As caretakers of history, we are required to ensure that the objects in our collections last as long as possible. To do this, we take steps to house our collections properly, we keep them in the best environment we can manage, and we wear white cotton gloves when handling the objects. The other part of our job is to offer access to the collection. This, of course, flies in the face of preservation. The worst possible thing for longevity of collection objects is to allow them to be handled. Digital imaging projects are the next tools for trying to solve the conflict that exists between offering access to our collections while at the same time protecting them for future generations.

PAST SOLUTIONS

In the past, particularly with photograph and manuscript collections, microfilming, photocopying, and making copies of photographic prints were used to provide access. Creating these surrogate copies allowed us to keep the originals safe and meet researchers' needs. But have these methods worked? Microfilming is a well-accepted tool for access. In fact, it is one of the few nationally accepted methods considered a preservation and access tool. Most newspaper collections around the United States are held as microfilm, the originals destroyed after filming was complete. Many manuscript collections are also filmed, particularly if they are in fragile condition.

Photographs and other graphically based collections do not translate well to microfilm. In the late 1980s, the Nebraska State Historical Society (NSHS) in partnership with the Kansas State Historical Society (KSHS) created a visual catalog of their most significant photograph collections. The project, funded by the National Endowment for the Humanities, resulted in high-quality tonal microfiche of more than one hundred thousand images. This catalog of images has offered tremendous access to the photograph collections from Nebraska and Kansas. The microfiche is available through interlibrary loan and has been used by researchers around the world. Researchers working in the reference room at the NSHS are required to use the microfiche first before they may look at originals. In many cases they never handle the originals at all, their needs being met by the microfiche.

Microfilm and microfiche sound like great solutions. There is still no better cost-effective way to preserve the information held in newspapers. And these film and fiche copies of the collections do protect originals from being handled. Microfilm and microfiche do not need refreshment cycles. They do not need computer software to access the information they hold. All they need is a light source and a magnifier.

The drawbacks when using this technology, however, are enormous. Three-dimensional objects do not translate well to the two-dimensional space of microfilm or microfiche. Graphic materials, such as photographs, broadsides, and paintings, are often much diminished in information content when converted to this media. Both microfilm and microfiche generate an image often smaller than the size of a quarter. Viewing machines enlarge these images; however, the larger they are projected, the more the information breaks down. Although it is possible, as with the NSHS and KSHS project, to generate high-quality tonal film and fiche, the image quality cannot compare to direct digital capture from the original. The film and fiche do not have the tonal range necessary to capture grayscale graphics adequately. Another drawback is color. Microfilm and microfiche are grayscale reproductions. If any of your material carries a color value, that information is lost in the filming process.

The other tool used extensively to generate copies from photographs and other graphic collections was the creation of copy negatives. To supply patrons with copy prints for research or for sale, copy negatives were generated from the original prints. Simply photographing the original object and then making a print from the resulting negative created the necessary copy. The copy print is then two generations removed from the original:

1. Original object → 2. New negative → 3. Copy print

The more steps required to create a copy print, the more degradation to the information. Again, in most cases any color value in the original was lost because the costs of black-and-white copy prints are much less than color. Copy negatives and prints remain quite expensive, especially if done properly as 4 × 5 inch negatives.

DIGITAL IMAGING AS THE NEW SOLUTION

Digital imaging is the new tool for offering access to collection material while at the same time helping preserve the originals. However, it is important to note that no matter how good the digital version of your original, it will never replace the experience of seeing the real thing. Each year digital technology advances,

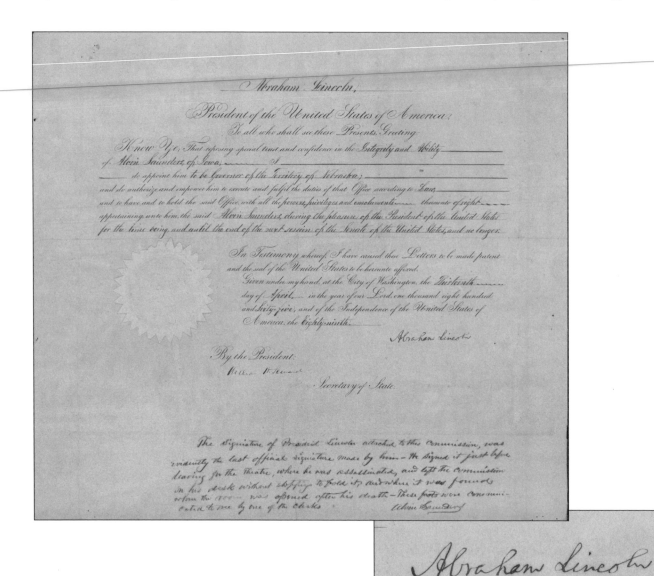

Figures 2.1 and 2.2   This document was found on Abraham Lincoln's desk the morning after his assassination. It appoints Alvin Saunders territorial governor of Nebraska. NSHS, Museum Collections, 606P.

but looking at an original document signed by Abraham Lincoln just prior to his assassination will never be superseded by looking at a digital copy online (see figures 2.1 and 2.2). Digital imaging can, however, provide copies of original objects far superior to those created by any technology available to date.

Undertaking a digital project will require much decision making. Before you begin, take a look at these four questions:

1. Is this project about access or preservation or both?
2. Which collections should be digitized?
3. Who is going to do the work?
4. How are you going to use these image files once the project is complete?

How you answer these questions will greatly affect the type of project you do, the time your project will take, the number of staff needed, the cost of the project, and the possible pitfalls you may encounter. If you are already in the midst of digitization, answering these questions may help you streamline your efforts.

1. Is This Project about Access or Preservation or Both?

A digital project designed purely as an access tool will be cheaper, take less time, and require less storage space for the image files, while a preservation project will be more expensive, take considerably more time, and need much more space for storage of files. Access projects generate small image files that hold less information and thus result in fewer uses. Preservation projects generate large image files that contain much more information and thus can be used in many more ways and for a much longer period of time. A preservation project will accomplish all the goals of an access project with many more advantages. Remember, if you are considering a project strictly for use on the Internet, files that can be posted and quickly downloaded on today's websites are much smaller than those that will be available to Internet users in the future. Why spend the time, effort, and money to create files only for use on today's Internet? It is well worth the effort to stick by the slogan "Scan once; scan right; scan for the future."

Here is a chart outlining the pros and cons of projects designed for access and those designed for preservation:

Access Projects
Benefits
Cheaper
Faster production times
Smaller storage requirements

Drawbacks
Smaller image files
Less information
Shorter life span

Image File Uses
Websites
CD-ROM publication
Easy accessibility on servers, PCs, and CD-ROMs

Preservation Projects
Benefits
Larger image files
Much more information
Extended life span

Drawbacks
More expensive
Slower production times
Larger storage requirements

Image File Uses
Limited only by pixel dimensions
Websites
CD-ROMs
Books, films, videos
Apparel
Postcards, posters, virtually anything

The term *preservation* is tricky when applied to digital imaging. In fact, it is a controversial issue. There is no such thing as preservation scanning in the sense that there is preservation microfilming. Digitization does not qualify as a nationally recognized tool for preservation as does microfilming. This is because of the very nature of digital imaging, the fact that computer hardware and software are required to access the information in the image files. Microfilm requires no such devices. Without the appropriate hardware and software, digital image files are just so much junk.

So what is a preservation digital project? The most important thing about a preservation digital project is that it aims to capture as much information as possible from the original object before that information is lost due to deterioration. We all know that despite our best efforts, collections continue to deteriorate. That is the nature of all things. We have taken the objects in our collections out of their normal use cycle: The object was made, it was used, and it was discarded. We step in somewhere before the discarding and begin an endless struggle to keep the object "alive." Some materials are more difficult than others, especially brittle paper, nitrate negatives, cellulose-based objects, leather, and silk. The point of preservation digital projects is to capture the information held by the original before time turns that information to dust.

For example, figure 2.3 is a glass plate negative taken by Solomon D. Butcher in 1889 of the Pacific Hotel in Callaway, Nebraska. As you can see by the first image, the glass is broken in three places; note the black lines going vertically across the image. The black holes in the roof and sky to the left of the turret are black because sections of the emulsion, the part of a photograph that holds the picture, are missing. These pieces of emulsion tore away and were lost after the glass broke.

Missing emulsion on the roof and sky may not seem

that important, but the break goes all the way across the plate, which is actually in three pieces, and the danger of losing more emulsion, particularly down by the porch of the hotel where several people are standing, is immediate and very likely if the original plate is continually accessed.

Notice the curved black line just above the porch in figure 2.4. This line is caused by a split or crack in the emulsion. If this negative is ever scanned again, there is a very real possibility that split will grow and the emulsion will completely separate from the rest of the image. Luckily for the NSHS, a print existed that was made from the glass negative prior to the break. (See figure 2.5.)

Figure 2.6 is another example of emulsion loss on a glass plate negative where no other copy exists. In fact, the plate is in one piece, but the emulsion is completely detached and was put back together much like a jigsaw puzzle to create this scan. Approximately six separate pieces of emulsion are completely detached from the glass.

Emulsion loss in photograph collections is only one type of information loss. Figure 2.7 is a letter written by

Figure 2.3   NSHS RG2608.PH-3443a.

Figure 2.4   Close-up of NSHS RG2608.PH-3443a.

Figure 2.5   Printing out paper print, or POP, c. 1920 from the original glass plate prior to the break, NSHS RG2608.PH-3443a.

Figure 2.6   NSHS Archives Photograph Teaching Collections.

Uriah Olbinger to his future wife, Mattie Thomas, on May 11, 1864. You can see from the image file that the original letter is in poor condition. It is actually in many pieces and was placed on an acid-free board with the pieces upright for digitization. This image file was generated using a Phase One FX digital scanback mounted on a Toyo view camera. Because of the fragile nature of the letter and the fact that it is in so many pieces, it was impossible to invert in order to digitize using a flatbed scanner, so the FX was used to capture the letter digitally from above.[1]

Properly done digital imaging projects can stop the loss of information over time. With careful attention to establishing benchmarks and extra care taken during the digitization process so no additional damage occurs, it is possible to retire the original objects with re-strictions for access, thereby extending their life for future generations.

2. Which Collections Should Be Digitized?

It may seem a silly question, but in reality, deciding which collections deserve digitization can be a tricky business. Not all collections are created equal, and not all collections should be digitized. But deciding where to start can sometimes be tough. There are conflicting opinions among staff, determined board members who like certain collections best, excited volunteers who just want to scan, researchers who only want easier access to your materials, and the list goes on of people who will give you suggestions for a digital project.

Make sure you do not limit yourself when consider-

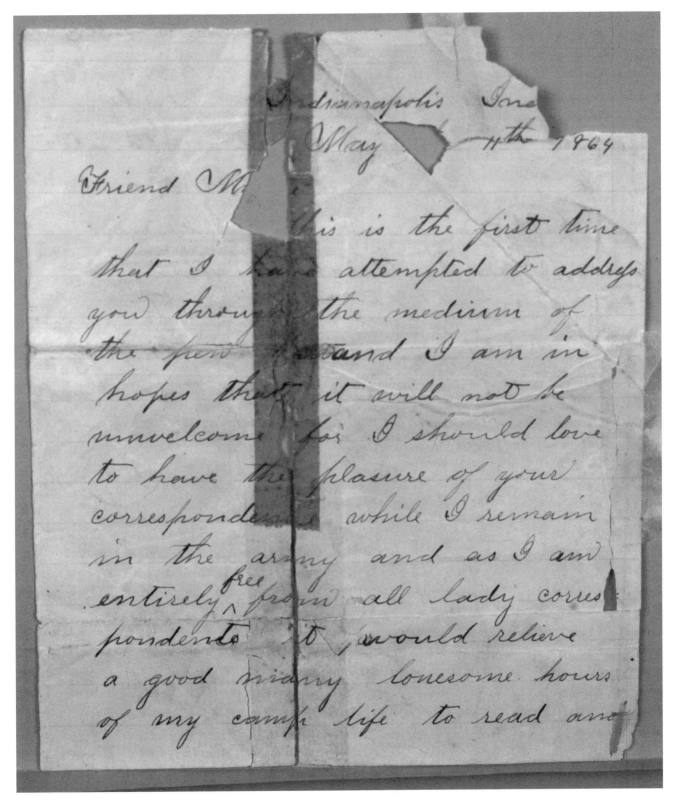

Figure 2.7   NSHS RG1346.AM.S01.L009, page 1.

ing what to digitize. Photographs and text-based collections are often the most obvious choices; however, three-dimensional collections can be digitized as well. What you really need is a tool that will help you make a clear, informed, and strong decision. You need a collection survey.

Collection surveys have been around for quite some time. They are used primarily as tools for gathering general information on a variety of topics about the collection. Digital imaging projects are just another use to which collection survey data can be put.

To conduct a collection survey, you must first determine the kind of information you want to record. For example, is there acquisition information about the collection? Who actually owns the collection if the institution does not? How well is it organized? Is any catalog information already in place? Collection surveys can help you identify serious problems like condition, pest infestations, and issues with donors. They are also a great way to capture brief subject information about the material. This will help you get an overall sense of the subjects where your collections are strong and, of course, weak.

The most helpful collection survey categories rank collections based on value and demand. These two factors are extremely important when determining which collection to choose for a digital project. Value is not a financial estimate. Giving a collection a high value is an indication of its historical worth. How well does this collection fit your collecting mission? How dense or detailed is the information in the collection? More information generally means more historical significance. Demand is based on how frequently researchers access the collection. This is tricky because if you have a great collection that has not yet been cataloged so researchers do not know it exists and therefore do not ask for it, the collection would get a low demand rating. However, in this circumstance, the value ranking would be high, so the collection might still be considered an option for digitization. Value and demand rankings are often best identified as high value/low value and high demand/low demand.

Conducting a collection survey may seem like a daunting task; however, it does not have to be, and it will look good on grant applications when you have to justify your decisions about which collection was chosen for digitization. The following sections offer some suggestions for setting up a collection survey. This information is based on collection surveys created by staff in the Library/Archives division of the NSHS for a National Historical Publications and Records Commission (NH-PRC) grant. Ultimately this information should reside in a database, but for purposes of gathering the information, it is much easier to do it on paper first.[2]

Collection Survey Field List

IDENTIFICATION DATA

At the beginning of your survey, you will want to record information that allows you to identify what is being surveyed. The easiest way to do this is by recording the collection number and name. You may decide to survey only a portion of the collection, in which case you need a field to identify which portion of the collection was surveyed. Since the value and demand rankings are so important to the decision-making process for digital projects, you may wish to include those two fields in this section as well.

Collection number
Collection name
Portion
Value: High/low
Demand: High/low

DESCRIPTIVE DATA

The fields used in this section of the survey depend entirely on the type of catalog data used by your institution. If no catalog data exists for any of your material, determine what type of catalog data will serve you and your patrons best, and then gather data based on those criteria. For any digital imaging project, especially one funded through a national grant, catalog data is required.

Collection-level description: Yes/no, automated/ manual
Group- or series-level description: Yes/no, automated/ manual
Item-level description: Yes/no, automated/manual
Other: Use a text field to describe any additional types of descriptive material that may exist—for example, information about the collection content found in donor records or collection files or bits of paper describing the collection and found with the collection itself.

Description status: Adequate/inadequate

Comments: It is often a good idea to give yourself plenty of space for additional comments, if you choose to take the time to record any.

ARRANGEMENT DATA

Arrangement is just what it sounds like. How is the collection organized, and is the organization adequate? Gathering this data will help you determine how much time it will take to prepare the collection for digitization. Note: If there is no arrangement, preparation time will be substantial and may cut too far into your project time line to finish digitization.

Fully arranged: Yes/no

Partially arranged: Yes/no

No arrangement: Yes/no

Arrangement status: Adequate/inadequate

Comments: Again, you may wish to include a comments field to allow for additional explanation of the arrangement status.

CONDITION DATA

This information is very important and will have a direct impact on any digitization of the collection. Objects that are in poor condition or are determined to be at risk (on the verge of complete loss) should be digitized first. However, they will undoubtedly require special handling and possible conservation treatment prior to digitization. Such steps will automatically increase the time line for your project.

Good: Yes/no

Poor: Yes/no

At risk: Yes/no

Comments: Describing the specific condition of the collection is vital when either "Poor" or "At Risk" apply.

HOUSING DATA

How the collections are stored or "housed" may help you find ways to add more matching funds to your grant application. If the collection you decide to digitize is not properly housed, include funds for new housing material in your budget. Make those funds "match" for the grant; that is, your institution buys the rehousing materials, rather than grant money.

Good: Yes/no

Poor: Yes/no

At risk: Yes/no

Comments: Describing the specific housing problems encountered will help you more quickly determine how to solve the problem without having to reexamine the collection.

SECURITY RISKS

A security risk exists if any portion of the collection has substantial financial or collectible value. For example, does your collection contain a letter signed by anyone famous? What about first edition books, original movie posters, or autographed baseballs? Many things are now considered quite collectible, and, thanks to online auction companies, prices for historic memorabilia have risen dramatically over the last several years. It is a good idea, whether doing a digital project or not, to know where in your collections security risks may exist.

Security risk: Yes/no

Comments: Describe which item is at risk, why it is at risk, and exactly where in the collection it is housed.

BULK DATES

To get a better sense of the general date span of your collection, consider including a section in your survey for bulk dates. These are dates represented by a majority of the collection. If the collection contains objects from 1900 through 1940, but a majority of the material was created in 1920 and there are only a few things from those other time periods, the bulk date would be 1920. Create yes/no fields for bulk dates by decade—for example, 1860, 1870, and 1880. If you intend to continue to gather survey data on new acquisition materials, include decades up to the present.

REGION

Gathering data about region will depend entirely on the scope of your collecting mission. This is general information, so if your collections relate solely to a single town, this field may not be necessary. However, if the collection covers an entire county, consider creating regions for each town or precinct. Create yes/no fields for regions that best suit your needs. The goal here is to determine what geographic areas the majority of your collections cover.

Collection surveys are particularly helpful for gathering general subject information. This is a key area for helping determine which collection to digitize first. However, keep in mind this is general subject data, not cataloging for access purposes. Be careful not to take too much time filling in subject information. Look at the collection as a whole and ask, "What is this about?" That will be your subject. Keep this field limited to five subjects at most. That will help you focus on the main topics.[3]

Collection surveys offer a great way to choose an appropriate topic or collection for a digital project. They give you statistical information that can prove to your board, the granting agency, and your users that the collection you've chosen is appropriate.

3. Who Is Going to Do the Work?

Once you have decided which collection to digitize, the next decision is who will do the work. This may seem to have an obvious answer: "We will." However, in-house digitization has disadvantages that are not always readily apparent. Do not rule out finding a vendor to do the digitization without first looking at the pros and cons of both scenarios. In-house production and outsourcing both have advantages and disadvantages. The key is to pick the solution that best suits your institution and your budget.

Outsourcing

Hiring an outsourcing vendor has several advantages: First, there are no up-front costs for purchasing scanners or other digital capture equipment. It will be necessary, however, for your institution to purchase a computer that can use the digital product being produced by your vendor. Second, not buying a scanner will make it unnecessary to incur the costs of keeping the equipment in working condition or replacing equipment as it becomes obsolete. Scanning technology is changing so rapidly that most scanners become obsolete within just a few years. Third, the project budget will not need to include hiring staff who know the intricacies of scanning software in order to digitize the collection. Even better, existing staff will not need to sideline other work in order to learn how to operate the scanner. Fourth, project staff

can concentrate their resources on cataloging and accessing the images once they are digitized. It will still be important, however, for project staff to have a good understanding of the technical issues related to digitization. This is particularly relevant for quality control checks on the vendor's product.

The disadvantages to outsourcing are also important. How far will your collections need to travel to the vendor? Can they be shipped safely? Several shipping companies in the United States deal exclusively in shipping art and artifacts, so for most historic materials, shipping can be done relatively safely. However, the cost is significant. Moving a collection, even from one room to another, is always a risk. Some vendors will bring their equipment to you. This is a happy alternative to shipping your collection.

If digitization is happening off-site, there will be a delay in quality control. Any contract you sign with an outsourcing vendor should include stipulations for achieving the benchmarks you define. Negotiations with the vendor should include a trial run that allows the vendor and your institution to verify the vendor can meet your benchmarks prior to signing a contract. It is also important to include weekly or biweekly shipments of files, so you can be assured the vendor is meeting your benchmarks on a regular basis. You do not want to end up with one large file shipment at the end of digitization and discover the vendor has made an error. Although the vendor should do quality control checks at its end, your project staff must do quality control as the files arrive.[4]

Other items to include in a vendor contract are as follows:

- Production rates—how many scans a week will the vendor produce?
- Rescanning conditions—how frequently will the vendor produce new scans if they are not meeting your benchmarks? How many bad scans are tolerated before the contract is void?

The main concern when hiring an outsourcing vendor is finding someone you trust. Many companies position themselves to offer digital imaging services to museums, libraries, and archives. These companies come in a variety of shapes and sizes and are definitely not all created equal. Just like any other service, you get what you pay for. Here is a checklist of things to ask when talking to a prospective vendor:

1. **Has the vendor ever digitized historic collections?** If the answer is yes, ask the vendor to describe the types of materials involved. Try to determine whether another cultural institution owned the material or whether it was a private family collection. Many companies will say they have digitized historic materials, but that usually means they have scanned old family photographs for private individuals. This does not mean they know how to handle historic material properly. Conservators around the country regularly see material that was damaged during the digitization process because vendors improperly handled the objects. If the company has worked for other museums, contact those previous clients for feedback about the vendor's work. Ask whether you can see examples of its image files.

   If the answer is no, the vendor has never worked with historic collections, you do not want to be its first attempt, so find another company.

2. **What type of equipment does the vendor use, including scanners, digital cameras, and computers?** Some scanning equipment can damage original materials, particularly if that material is brittle. Do not allow the use of document feeders or movable scanning beds with historic collections. The potential for damage is too great. A document feeder automatically sends the objects one at a time across the scanner bed, much like a copy machine. Most historic collection material will not tolerate the stress caused by this type of equipment. Movable scanning beds require the object be attached to the scanner so there is no movement of the object during digitization. Movable scan beds, such as drum scanners, offer very high resolution but are not acceptable for historic materials. Drum scanners require that the object wrap around a tube for digitization. Most historical collection material cannot stand this treatment without damage. Asking the vendor for its equipment specifications is often a required element for grant proposals. Knowing this information ahead of time will help you evaluate the equipment and make an informed decision as to whether it can generate files that will meet your benchmarks and at the same time protect your collection from damage.

3. **What type of media does the vendor use for file storage?** Although your institution will not be purchasing a scanner for your digital project, you will need to have the right hardware to use the image files created by your vendor. How will the vendor deliver your digital files? Zip disk, CD-ROM, DVD? Can the vendor generate the file format you need? Will those files be usable by anyone other than you and the vendor? Does the vendor intend to maintain a set of image files generated from your collection after the project is complete? Why? This might be an interesting option for off-site file backup. But do you trust the vendor not to use or distribute your image files, even among vendor staff?

4. **Will the vendor sign a contract stipulating your benchmarks for the image file creation?** This is vital and should not be a problem. If it is, find a new vendor.

5. **What type of metadata does the vendor create for the image files?** This question often weeds out vendors that have never worked with museum collections. Metadata is another major component of grant applications. Can the vendor generate metadata, information about the creation of the image file, for you? If not, it is possible to create some of the metadata after the fact. However, this adds the possibility of error and creates more work for your project staff. Consider including metadata standards in the contract you sign with the vendor.

6. **Who owns the files, you or the vendor?** To maintain ownership of the image files and therefore maintain control over your collection, be sure to include a statement in your contract that clarifies ownership. Your institution must own the image files, not the vendor.

7. **Where are the collections stored while at the vendor's facility?** Ask for a tour. How does it compare to your collection storage area? How stable is the HVAC system? Are there extreme fluctuations in humidity levels?

8. **What type of security is available?** Will the material be safe? Will the security measures in place be sufficient? The bottom line is, do you feel safe leaving your collection in the hands of this vendor?

9. **What type of fire suppression system exists in the vendor's facility?** Most businesses use sprin-

kler systems for fire suppression. Can the vendor take steps to protect your collection from water damage that may result if the fire system is activated? One idea is to transport your collection to the vendor using inert plastic tubs and request that the vendor always return collection material to those tubs at the end of each day. Another alternative is to wrap acid-free boxes in plastic and request the vendor keep the collection covered at all times when not being digitized. These measures will give some protection to your collection in the event of fire suppression activation.

10. **What responsibility, if any, will the vendor assume if your collection is damaged while at its facility?** It is not unusual for a vendor to assume no responsibility. Therefore, be assured the vendor knows how to handle and protect your one-of-a-kind collection properly. Ask the vendor to provide insurance if the materials are lost in a fire, flood, or other natural disaster.

Outsourcing requires clear communication between your institution and the vendor before and during digitization. Although risks are involved, outsourcing may be the best solution for your project. Remember: Buying, maintaining, and updating digitization equipment can be very costly and requires a long-term institutional commitment.

In-House Production

In-house production is by far the most popular choice among institutions beginning digital projects. This technology is fun and exciting, and people want to be involved on all levels, which is obviously why you are reading this book. But there are some serious long-term implications to consider. First, your institution will have to make a large initial investment in digitization equipment. Most grant agencies do not fund the purchase of equipment, so the money for scanners, computers, and software will have to be raised from another source. Once the initial digital project is complete, the scanner will still be there, and it is unlikely to become inactive. Most institutions continue to scan collections after their initial projects are complete. This is advantageous, but how are you going to pay for those scans through your regular budget? Can you afford that? And can you afford the staff time away from other duties? Do you want digitization to become a major priority for your institution?

Second, once a scanner and computer are purchased, someone must be responsible for maintaining and upgrading the equipment. Do you already have an information technology (IT) person on staff? Are you expecting the project director to assume that role for the digital project? What happens after the project is complete and that staff member must resume regular duties? How are you planning to fund maintenance and upgrades for the equipment? Can your institutional budget cover those costs, or will you need to seek private funding? If you were successful in getting private funding for the initial equipment purchase, can you return to that same funding source every few years to request money for upgrades or repairs? One way to raise money for upgrades and replacement of aging equipment is to put a portion of the revenue generated from the sale of digital images and use fees in a separate fund. This works quite well over an extended period of time, particularly if you charge patrons duplication service fees.

Third, with in-house production comes the need for staff and training. As mentioned earlier in the discussion about outsourcing, it is very important for project staff to understand digital technology in order to achieve high-quality scans. This knowledge comes into play in outsourcing projects through quality control of a vendor's product. With in-house projects, staff need not only to perform quality control but to clearly understand the intricacies of the scanning software in order to create high-quality scans. If your digital project utilizes one scanning technician to generate the scans, another staff member will be needed to perform quality control on the image files. It is not recommended that the person generating the initial files perform quality control on those files. At least two people are required for accurate quality control.[5]

Fourth, where will the project work take place? Do you have a spare office or spare section of a room that can become your digital imaging laboratory? This point may seem trivial, but in reality it is a vital part of the smooth work flow of any digital project. A clean work space needs to have not only plenty of room for the scanner and computer but also table space for the items being digitized. It may also be important to have extra room for dealing with items that require special attention, such as dirty glass plate negatives, deteriorating silk garments, or fragile broadsides. The area around the scanner and computer must be as clean as possible. Another factor to consider is that this space will be permanently lost to other projects. Once the scanner and computer are in place and operating effectively, it is not a good idea to move the scanner around. Although scanners are smaller and lighter than ever before, they still contain sensitive hardware that can easily be jostled out of alignment, causing malfunctions.

The two greatest benefits for in-house production are not having to move the collection outside your facility and getting immediate results from the digitization. There is also, of course, the satisfaction of gaining a deep understanding of digital technology and accomplishing the work yourself.

4. How Are You Going to Use These Image Files Once the Project Is Complete?

Most digital image projects are designed to create image files for use on websites, either within searchable databases or as online exhibits. There are, however, a multitude of uses for high-quality digital images of collection materials. Since you are going to the trouble of digitizing your collection, you should utilize the files in as many ways possible to get the most out of your investment.

Many collection management software packages are capable of importing digital images. This is particularly helpful for staff and volunteers who use such programs. Including an image of the object being described greatly increases the usefulness of the software. We are a visual culture and therefore respond more quickly to images than words.

If you do not use an off-the-shelf collections management software package, you can still benefit from linking your images to your collections data. Most current database packages are capable of importing image files directly into the database. Another alternative is to link to the image file, which is stored outside the database.[6]

High-quality digital image files can generate beautiful digital prints. New exhibits featuring digital prints show a marked improvement over their darkroom predecessors. In 2002, the Nebraska State Historical Society opened a new permanent exhibit titled "Building the State: Nebraska 1867–1916," with approximately two hundred photographs. All of them were generated from high-quality digital image files. As you walk through the gallery, the difference in quality is obvious compared to the prints on display in the other permanent exhibits. Prior to the "Building the State" exhibit, all photographic prints were created in a traditional darkroom. "Building the State" utilizes digital prints that are sharper and contain much more detail. In some cases, contrast adjustment and sharpening filters made significant contributions to the effectiveness of the images.

CONCLUSION

Digital image files offer unlimited access to your collection. Rather than having to decide which collection objects to display in a given space, use a computer to offer access to your entire collection electronically. This can be accomplished in a very small area within an exhibit gallery, a research room, or simply your front office. Once your collection is digitized, your ability to share knowledge with others increases exponentially.

NOTES

1. For more information on digital cameras, see chapter 6, "Choosing Equipment."
2. For more information on databases, see chapter 7, "How to Track Digital Image Files: Metadata and Databases."
3. For information on using subject headings, see chapter 7.
4. For more information on establishing benchmarks and conducting quality control, see chapter 5, "Technical Specifications."
5. For more information on staffing needs and duties, see chapter 4, "Project Management."
6. For more information on databases, see chapter 7.

CHAPTER 3

Ethics and Copyright

BEFORE BEGINNING A DIGITAL IMAGING PROJECT, IT IS very important to understand and adhere to a set of ethical principles and clear any issues of copyright. Ethics is important to digital imaging projects because it is so easy to misrepresent an original and copy, manipulate, and distribute digital files. Copyright is crucial because you do not want to put you or your institution at risk of copyright violations that can lead not just to embarrassment but to lawsuits.

ETHICS

Ethics and digital imaging are inextricably linked. Because it is so easy for anyone to manipulate an image file, even if his or her intention is not malicious, your institution should establish a code of ethics associated with the creation, manipulation, and distribution of those files. If you have written policy in place, it will go a long way toward authenticating your image files and establishing your institution as a credible source for historic materials.

Manipulation is the most volatile issue surrounding digital imaging ethics. With today's powerful image manipulation software, it only takes a few seconds to alter a digital file radically. Two clicks of the mouse are all that is necessary to flip the photograph depicted in figures 3.1 and 3.2. Four minutes was all it took to remove one of the people in the image (figure 3.3). Who could tell which image file accurately represents the original? Once in the digital arena, it becomes impossible to know which file is authentic to the original object. That is why a digital imaging code of ethics is so important.

To date, there is no standard code of digital imaging ethics that can be adopted by those of us creating digital image files. Perhaps we should take a lesson from the members of the American Institute for Conservation of Historic and Artistic Works (AIC). Every conservator who belongs to this national organization works under the *AIC Code of Ethics and Guidelines for Practice.*[1] This document is meant as a guarantee that the conservator works at the highest standards to achieve the goal of preservation of cultural property. It may seem overkill to suggest ethics for digital imaging, particularly when staff of the institution that owns the originals generates the files. However, adhering to a code of ethics adds a layer of authenticity to the digital image files. The code of ethics should stipulate the way in which the files are generated and how those files are monitored and state that no damage was done to the original objects in order to achieve the digital copy. It is also important to include language that clarifies acceptable and unacceptable manipulation. Be sure to state that no manipulation is allowed on master image files. Manipulation is the key element in a code of ethics document. Clarification here will help validate the reliability of your image files. If a researcher questions the authenticity or content of an image file, your code of ethics document can help relieve any doubts that what a researcher sees in your digital version of a collection object is real.

If your institution is large enough to have several staff members or divisions working with collections, consider including information in the code of ethics giving a staff member or division ultimate responsibility for the files. Note: In some cases, digital image files are generated from noncollection material—for example, maps or illustrations created by staff for exhibition purposes and then digitized for print publication or website use. Be sure to cover in your code of ethics whether or not these files will get the same treatment as image files generated from collection materials.

COPYRIGHT

Copyright is often confusing and difficult to understand. The advent of digital technology has made that confusion more widespread. If you have copyright concerns, you should seek the advice of a copyright attorney. The information provided here is not meant as legal advice. The intent here is to provide tools that describe copyright and examples of what some museums and libraries are doing to protect the copyright of their websites.

Figure 3.1　NSHS RG2608.PH-1004.

Figure 3.2　NSHS RG2608.PH-1004, digitally altered.

Figure 3.3   NSHS RG2608.PH-1004, digitally altered.

The basic question for any institution working on a digital project is this: Does your institution have the right to copy (and a scan is a copy) the item you are digitizing? To make that determination, it must first be decided whether the item is protected by copyright. Property right is not the same as copyright. Your institution may own the *item* but not the *copyright* for that item. For example, many studio photographers maintain copyright of the photographs they create. Your institution may own a set of family photographs taken by a studio; however, the family does not own the copyright and cannot transfer copyright to your institution upon donation. The photography studio maintains the copyright. This means you cannot make copies of studio portraits without the permission of the studio that took the photographs.

So how can copyright be determined? Table 3.1 is a very useful chart created by Professor Laura N. Gasaway, the director of Law Library and a professor of law at the University of North Carolina, Chapel Hill. First determine when the items were created. Then plug those dates into Professor Gasaway's chart to determine whether they are under copyright. This chart is used with permission and can be found online at

www.unc.edu/~unclng/public-d.htm. Professor Gasaway recommends that you check this site for updates to the chart as copyright law continues to evolve.

Public domain means that no individual owns copyright. Anything published before 1923 is now in the public domain. You may scan without fear of violating copyright. If an item was created before 1923 but never published, copyright is held by the creator for the lifetime of the creator plus seventy years or until December 31, 2002, whichever is greater. For example, the Nebraska State Historical Society (NSHS) has an extensive collection of unpublished manuscripts and photographs that were created between 1909 and 1970 by a woman named Margaret Gehrke. The materials in this collection will fall into the public domain seventy years after her death, which occurred in 1978. This material will be in public domain in 2048, rather than falling into public domain on December 31, 2002, because the lifetime of the creator plus seventy years is longer than December 31, 2002.

Note: Even if the creator is deceased heirs can still hold copyright. To digitize Margaret Gehrke's collection, staff at the Nebraska State Historical Society

Table 3.1   Copyright Chart

| | WHEN WORKS PASS INTO THE PUBLIC DOMAIN[1] | |
DATE OF WORK	PROTECTED FROM	TERM
Created 1/1/78 or after	When work is fixed in tangible medium of expression	Life + 70 years[2] (or if work of corporate authorship, the shorter of 95 years from publication or 120 years from creation[3])
Published before 1923	In public domain	None
Published from 1923–1963	When published with notice[4]	28 years + could be renewed for 47 years, now extended by 20 years for a total renewal of 67 years. If not so renewed, now in public domain
Published from 1964–1977	When published with notice	28 years for first term; now automatic extension of 67 years for second term
Created before 1/1/78 but not published	1/1/78, the effective date of the 1976 act which eliminated common law copyright	Life + 70 years or 12/31/2002, whichever is greater
Created before 1/1/78 but published between then and 12/31/2002	1/1/78, the effective date of the 1976 act which eliminated common law copyright	Life + 70 years or 12/31/2047, whichever is greater

1. By Laura N. Gasaway, University of North Carolina, last updated September 18, 2001; notes courtesy of professor Tom Field, Franklin Pierce Law Center.
2. Term of joint works is measured by life of the longest-lived author.
3. Works for hire, anonymous, and pseudonymous works also have this term (17 U.S.C. § 302[c]).
4. Under the 1909 Act, works published without notice went into the public domain upon publication. Works published without notice between 1/1/78 and 3/1/89, effective date of the Berne Convention Implementation Act, retained copyright only if, for example, registration was made within five years (17 U.S.C. § 405).

contacted her only living relative to request permission to digitize and eventually publish the material.

Putting your materials to the copyright test will undoubtedly turn up items chosen for your digital project that still have copyright restrictions. To include these items in your project, you must make a reasonable effort to clear copyright. In other words, your institution must do whatever it can to get permission from the copyright holder to digitize and utilize those files. This can be extremely difficult and often time-consuming, so you might consider pulling the items from digitization. The NSHS faced this issue when working on its first digital imaging project.[2] One half of the project involved digitizing and SGML-tagging over six thousand pages of letters.[3] Much of this material was written prior to 1923; however, the author's life–plus–seventy–years rule kept the material out of the public domain. The decision was made to write a letter to as many of the author's descendants as NSHS staff were able to find. The letter included an enthusiastic description of the project and a request for feedback from the descendants if they had doubts or concerns about the letters being posted on the Internet. All those who responded to the letter were excited about the project and appreciated our efforts to contact them.

Copyright as a Tool for Protecting Your Collection

It is important to protect the integrity of your collection, especially once mounted on a website. You may accomplish this goal in two ways. One is through watermarking the image files; the other is copyright.[4] Copyright notices come in many forms. They can apply to individual image files, individual pages of text, groups of images and text, or entire websites. Using a copyright statement implies you are claiming the authority to authorize others to reproduce the content, distribute copies, or display the material publicly. U.S. Copyright law, title 17 of the *U.S. Code*, grants ownership of copyright to the original creators of the work.

It is standard practice in the museum and archive profession to copyright websites. A copyright statement on your website protects the site much as the copyright on a book protects the book. Most museum and archive websites include a standard copyright statement, sometimes on every page of the site—for example, "© 2003 Nebraska State Historical Society, All Rights Reserved." Some copyright statements link to a page with expanded copyright information. The NSHS copyright statement is quite specific about what you can and cannot do with the material on the site. It also links to a more extended information page about license fee requirements. The Denver Public Library Western History Collection copyright statement includes a sentence claiming copyright to the digital image files on the site. Presented here are the copyright pages listed on the websites of the Nebraska State Historical Society and the Denver Public Library. (This material is reproduced with permission.)

Nebraska State Historical Society

Copyright © 1998–2003 by the Nebraska State Historical Society, Lincoln, Nebraska. All rights reserved.

The photographs, graphics, texts, and other materials on this site are supplied by the Nebraska State Historical Society for personal, research, and nonprofit educational purposes only. Permission to reproduce these in any form, other than for individual and educational use, must be obtained in writing from the Nebraska State Historical Society (more information below).

Responsibility regarding questions of copyright, photographic releases, and invasion of privacy that may arise from such use are assumed by the user.

Copyright for some material(s) on these pages may be held by others. The transmission or reproduction of these protected items, beyond that of fair use, requires the written permission of the copyright owner(s). Additionally, copyright on other historical materials appearing here may be difficult or impossible to determine; nevertheless, determinations of appropriate use are the responsibility of the user.

Conditions for use of digital material:

The right to use digital materials from the Nebraska State Historical Society is granted to individuals and nonprofit educational institutions on a one-time use only basis, with the following conditions:

1. That proper citation be used. Unless more specifically stated with the page, text, image, or graphic, citation must always minimally read: "Nebraska State Historical Society." The purpose of citation is twofold: for proper credit, and to allow others to find and verify the information being cited. Complete citation includes, if applicable: author or photographer, title or image number, the URL, and the date. See the sample citations for each type of information.
2. That there is no misrepresentation of the images,

recordings, text, or other material so as to falsify the information they present.
3. That the user assumes responsibility for all questions concerning copyright violation, invasion of privacy, slander, and/or libel resulting from the use of the texts, images, or recordings.
4. That no manipulation of any kind be made to a Nebraska State Historical Society digital image file(s) without written permission from the Nebraska State Historical Society. Manipulation includes but is not limited to the following: contrast adjustments, rotation, inversion, sharpness, tonal adjustments, resolution, and removal or alteration, in any manner, of details inherent to the original image.

In addition, commercial users must sign an agreement to the following conditions:

1. That any applicable use fee required by the Society be paid upon completion of the project. To receive information about our fees, see the fee schedule on this site, or to find out if commercial fees are applicable, contact us at 402-471-4751.
2. That a copy of the product in which Nebraska State Historical Society images, recordings, text, or other materials were used be provided to the Society at no cost (this condition may be waived, subject to approval of a written request submitted to the Society's director). If the product is a posting on another electronic site accessible by the public, the URL shall be forwarded to the staff handling the agreement.

For More Information about Copyright, Use, and Digital Imaging:

1. Concerning use and use fees, contact reference services at 402-471-4751.
2. Concerning digital imaging and graphics, see Digital Imaging, or contact the curator of photographs at 402-471-4409 or koelling@nebraska history.org.
3. Concerning copyright and information about textual information on this website, contact the editor at 402-471-4747.
4. About linking to the Nebraska State Historical Society pages, and the use of Society graphics other than photographs, contact the webmaster at 402-471-4766.

DISCLAIMER

This site is dedicated to the idea of an open dialogue concerning the past. The opinions expressed in interpretive materials are not necessarily those of the Nebraska State Historical Society, but are those of the authors or creators of the material.

Some of the historical materials on this site may contain negative, inappropriate, or offensive connotations reflective of a culture or language of a period or place in our past. These materials are presented here as part of the historical record.

Denver Public Library, Western History Collection

Copyright Notice

The Denver Public Library is unaware of any copyright in the images in the collection. We encourage use of these materials under the fair use clause of the 1976 copyright act. All images in this collection may be used for educational, scholarly purposes, and private study. We do request that a credit line be included with each item used.

If you wish to publish or reproduce the material in any physical or digital form that exceeds that permitted by fair use or use them for any commercial purpose, including display or web page use, you must obtain prior written permission from the Denver Public Library, The Colorado Historical Society, or the Denver Art Museum.

For information on prices, policies, and purchasing of any Denver Public Library image, please contact our Photo Sales Department or call (720) 865-1818.

For information on prices, policies, and purchasing prints of any Colorado Historical Society image (items with call numbers beginning with "CHS") click here.

For information on prices, policies, and purchasing prints of any Denver Art Museum image (items with call numbers beginning with "DAM") click here.

The Denver Public Library has provided in the catalog records for these materials all known information regarding the photographer or other persons associated with the materials. This information is provided as a service to aid customers in determining the appropriate use of an item, but that determination ultimately rests with the customer.

The nature of historical archival photograph collections means that copyright or other information about restrictions may be difficult or even impossible to determine. The Denver Public Library would like to hear from anyone who may have additional information regarding the images found in this collection.

This site uses the CARLWEB search engine. Copyright 1997–2001 Carl Corporation.[6]

The point of most digital projects is to make available to a wider audience the wonderful material in our collections. It is not our intent to infringe on copyright. Consider including such a statement on your website and with any printed material associated with the results of your digital project. The Denver Public Library includes the statement "The Denver Public Library would like to hear from anyone who may have additional information regarding the images found in this collection."[7] This is a very good idea because it states to all of your patrons your interest in their knowledge, and it may garner you important information about your collection.

LICENSE CONTRACTS

Aside from copyright statements, consider adopting license contracts for some or all patrons who use your collection. Asking patrons to sign a contract agreeing to specific rules regarding the use of your collections enforces your ability to control use. This is very important in the digital age. License contracts, like digital watermarks, do not keep thieves from robbing you, but they do show your patrons you are making a concerted effort to protect the integrity of your collections, and that is a vital part of most institutional mission statements.

License contracts are as varied as the institutions that

Box 3.1   Sample License 1

Photograph Use Permission Form[1]
UTAH STATE HISTORICAL SOCIETY

Photograph Use Policy

Written permission from the Utah State Historical Society is required to use Society images for any purpose other than private research or strictly personal use. All such uses require the following credit: ***Used by permission, Utah State Historical Society, all rights reserved.*** There is no charge for use of photos for private or noncommercial educational purposes. There is a licensing charge for commercial/business use of images. This charge will vary depending on the intended use. (See licensing charge schedule.) The Historical Society also requests (but does not require) the donation of a copy of the product in which the image is used.

To obtain permission to use images it is necessary to fill out this form and pay all applicable charges. The funds collected are used for preservation and expansion of the collection.

Warranties and Disclaimer

The Utah State Historical Society represents and warrants that the photographs or images in the collection were gifted or granted to the Society, that pursuant to the gift or grant the Society has a right to act with respect to such photograph or image, and that as far as the Society is aware, but without investigation, the rights granted by it hereunder will not infringe the rights of any third party. Notwithstanding the foregoing, the Society is acting as an owner of the physical image. The Society is not responsible for determining the copyright status of the photographs or images, nor for securing copyright permission or payment for any such permission as required. The rights granted under this agreement do not include any rights that persons other than the Society may have in the photographs or images, including any artist's rights of attribution or control under the laws of any country or state, moral rights, or the rights of publicity or privacy.

Rights Granted Back

The Society shall have and be granted a non-exclusive right to use, utilize, and publish the photographs or images as well as any derivative image produced by the Licensee, including copyrighted works and copyrighted derivative works of the Licensee.

Intended Use of Images

Use Charge per Image

_____ Commercial Use _____ Non-Commercial Use _____ Private Research / Personal Use

Please Describe:

I understand that permission for use of these images applies to one-time use as described above and that additional permission is required for any different or subsequent use.
I agree to abide by the policy stated above.

_____

Signature/Date

Subject to payment of applicable charges and compliance with all conditions stated above, permission for the above named use is herewith granted.

_____

Utah State Historical Society/Date

1. This information used with permission from the Utah State Historical Society, www.history.utah.gov/library/photoorder.html.

Box 3.2   Sample License 2

Nebraska State Historical Society[1]
Media Services License Agreement for Delivery and Use

This is a sample contract provided in order to explain the details associated with any type of use of NSHS archival materials. NSHS staff will send you a completed version of this contract when you place an order for copies from NSHS archival materials.

Agreement for Delivery and Use

I [user's name] understand that the Nebraska State Historical Society is providing a copy or copies of the objects listed on the attached sheet for the following use:

Type of Use [No Use Fee Required]

Research
Academic Lecture
Personal
Student Project or Paper
Other:_____

Type of Use [Fee Required]

Film/Video
Broadcast
Home Video/DVD
Advertisement
Production for Theatrical Release

Print Media
Book
Poster
Serial
Book Jacket
Calendar or Greeting Card

Electronic Media
Website
CDR/DVD

Other
Non-broadcast
Live public presentation
On-site exhibition
Other: _____

____ All Media
Distribution: ____ World
                     ____ One Country
                     ____ One Language
                     ____ All Languages

Title: _____

Number of copies _____
I agree to abide by the following conditions:

Adherence to Use

The attached listed copy(ies) of materials from the collections of the Nebraska State Historical Society will be considered for non-exclusive one-time use only in the publication, project, production, or personal use detailed on this agreement. I understand that any additional or alternate uses, including but not limited to subsequent editions, reprints, re-releases, dust jackets, covers, print or broadcast advertisement, companion formats, and distribution in other markets, constitute a new use which must be documented and approved by the Nebraska State Historical Society.

Fair Use

I confirm that I am aware of the portion of the copyright law of the United States (Title 17, United States Code), which governs the making of photocopies or other reproductions of copyrighted material, summarized as follows:

Under certain conditions specified in the law, libraries and archives are authorized to furnish a photocopy or other reproduction. One of these specified conditions is that the photocopy or other reproduction is not to be "used for any purpose other than private study, scholarship, or research." If a user makes a request for, or later uses, a photocopy or reproduction for purposes in excess of "fair use" that user may be liable for copyright infringement. This institution reserves the right to refuse to accept a copying order if, in its judgment, fulfillment of the order would involve violation of copyright law.

Copyright, Libel, and Slander

I assume responsibility for any copyright violation, issues of invasion of privacy, libel, and/or slander that may result from my use of these materials.

Endorsement

I understand that the materials are not to be used to assert or imply that the Nebraska State Historical Society endorses any product or enterprise, concurs with the opinions expressed in, or confirms the accuracy of any content of the described publication, project, or production.

Identification/Credit Line

I agree to correctly identify the content of the materials provided by the Nebraska State Historical Society and to not use them in a way that falsifies or misrepresents the information they present. Furthermore, I agree to credit the Nebraska State Historical Society for the materials used in completed paper or project as follows: Nebraska State Historical Society, [insert type of collection] for example: RG0849.PH:9-21 Nebraska State Historical Society

Manipulation

I understand that, while the Nebraska State Historical Society will allow close-ups of portions of the original and adjustments to contrast, sharpness, and cropping where the original content is not changed, it will NOT allow inversion of the original or change in resolution of digital files, or the removal or addition of content. The Nebraska State Historical Society's primary interest is to protect the content of the original. The Nebraska State Historical Society may enhance the original material to allow for better interpretation and understanding of the content. I understand that any manipulation beyond that allowed by the Nebraska State Historical Society must be approved by the Nebraska State Historical Society in advance of use as an addendum to this agreement.

Passing Copies

I understand that the rights to the provided materials cannot be sub-leased or sold, nor may I permit others to reproduce the materials or any facsimiles of them by any means for any purpose. Likewise, I understand that these materials may not be donated or sold to another person or organization.

Destruction or Return of Electronic Media

I agree to DESTROY or RETURN to the Nebraska State Historical Society any copies of materials provided to me on electronic media by the Nebraska State Historical Society upon the completion of the project, publication, production, or personal use detailed in this agreement.

License Fee

I agree to pay a license fee not to exceed _____ [to be determined] to the Nebraska State Historical Society for use of the provided materials actually used in the final project, publication, or production. I understand that this fee is levied in addition to other processing and service charges associated with providing the copy(ies). I understand that this fee may be negotiated, upon my submission of a written justification to the Nebraska State Historical Society that supports my inability to pay the stated use fee.

A copy of the product, production, or project shall be provided to the Nebraska State Historical Society as part of the license agreement.
This contract is entered into in the jurisdiction of the State of Nebraska.

1. This information used with permission from the Nebraska State Historical Society, www.nebraskahistory.org/lib-arch/services/reference/sample.htm.

create them. Many museums have use agreement information on their websites. Boxes 3.1 and 3.2 are just two examples: contracts used by the Utah State Historical Society and the Nebraska State Historical Society. Always check the institution's website for updates to the contracts. In this age of copyright reform, changes occur regularly to contracts for use. Your institution should consider creating a contract that can be filled out online by a user and submitted electronically. This will save considerable staff time.

CONCLUSION

Addressing the issues of ethics and copyright prior to the start of a digital imaging project will prepare you for any tough questions you may face once your digitized material is available online. It will also go a long way toward convincing potential funders and users of your materials that you care about how historic materials are represented and protected for future generations.

NOTES

1. To see the complete *AIC Code of Ethics and Guidelines for Practice*, go to http://aic.stanford.edu/pubs/ethics .html.
2. For more information on this project, see the preface or go to the website http://memory.loc.gov/ammem/ award98/nbhihtml/pshome.html.
3. *SGML* stands for standard generalized markup language. It is a series of characters that helps a computer program understand the way the text should be displayed. HTML, or hypertext markup language, which is used to tell web browser software how to display a web page, is a subset of SGML.
4. For more information on watermarking, see chapter 1, "A Digital Glossary."
5. This information used with permission from the Nebraska State Historical Society.
6. This information used with permission from the Denver Public Library, http://gowest.coalliance.org/ copyright.html.
7. Denver Public Library Western History/Genealogy Department website, http://gowest.coalliance.org.

CHAPTER 4

Project Management

PROJECT MANAGEMENT INCLUDES NOT ONLY PLANNING your budget but also identifying staffing needs, defining your projects time line, and making your grant competitive. All of these issues are closely linked to creating a successful digital imaging project.

DEFINING YOUR BUDGET

There are several things to consider when defining a budget for a digital imaging project: How much will it cost to generate each scan? How much will the computers needed to use the scans cost? How many staff members will be needed to run the project? Will you need conservation treatment services? Will you need to purchase new housing materials? How soon will you have to start refreshment, and how much will it cost? Are you going to need additional prints or copies of the CDs? Answering these questions will frame the majority of your project budget and help you plan for the future.

If you decide to utilize an outsourcing company to do your digitization, you will have to budget for the cost. It is difficult to predict what the costs will be as the technology advances and more competition develops, but estimates can be based on the way costs are structured. Generally, an outsourcing company will charge by the scan for straight digitization from an original. After the scan cost will come costs for storage media, such as CD-ROMs, costs for file transfer to the storage media, costs for creating additional files or surrogate files, and, of course, costs for any manipulation to those surrogate files. Manipulation costs are usually charged at an hourly rate. Some companies may be willing to negotiate a rate reduction if you have a large number of scans to produce.

In-house digitization projects will require budgeting for the purchase of equipment. Costs of scanners continue to decline, but do not buy the cheapest scanner you can find. (For help in determining what to look for in a scanner, see chapter 6.) Scanner costs are highly dependent on their specifications. The speed of the scanner, or how many scans it can produce in an hour, will affect the cost, as will the dynamic range and the optical resolution. The faster the scanner, the higher the dynamic range, and the higher the optical resolution, the more expensive the scanner will be.

Costs for computers to run the scanner, burn CD-ROMs, or simply store image files will vary depending on processor speeds, hard drive storage space, and the size of the monitor. Most computers are now available with DVD drives, so you may consider adding an additional drive, internal or external, to burn CDs. It is possible to buy a computer with a DVD/CDRW combination drive. However, this will increase the price. Compare the cost of DVD/CDRW combination drives with external and internal CDRW drives to help make your decision. Every month new computers are available, and although costs do not decline, what you get for the cost does increase.

To determine how much each scan will cost, consider the following: How fast is your scanner? How many scans can it generate in an hour? How fast is your computer processor? This will impact the speed at which files open and can be duplicated, manipulated, and saved. How efficient are your scanning technicians? There will be a learning curve, of course, but once they are on track, how many scans can they generate per hour? Compare that figure to how much you are paying them per hour. Consider setting aside a percentage of your scan cost as funding for maintaining and upgrading your equipment.

Refreshment costs will not be a part of your initial project budget. The long-term budget of your institution must include costs for refreshment once a commitment to digital projects begins. As soon as you generate a digital image file, it enters a refreshment cycle. Refreshment is a key factor in any digital project and is worth the cost. You do not want to end up with image files that are not retrievable because they are on media you can no longer access. Refreshment costs will vary considerably as technology advances and therefore is hard to predict, but it will always be linked to staffing costs, computer processor speeds, and storage media costs.

Expendables such as prints, CDs, DVDs, phone calls, travel, and shipping your objects to an outsourcing vendor must all be included in your budget. Print costs will depend on the type of printer you use; they will vary from less than a dollar to close to three dollars each. CDs are now available for less than one dollar apiece if purchased in bulk. Expendables along with rehousing materials are often used as match in grant-funded digital imaging project budgets.

STAFFING NEEDS

Digital imaging projects require some very specific staffing needs. Many of these positions can be combined so fewer staff are required. But remember, if staff positions are combined, it will take longer to complete the entire process, which will affect not only the time line but the budget as well. At the minimum you need two people for a digital imaging project. One person can do everything, but then you have no quality control for digital image files or cataloging.

Skills required for digital imaging projects include the obvious: technical ability to operate computers and scanners, skills for proper handling of original source materials, and an interest in and knowledge of the collection to be digitized. It is also important for project staff to be highly motivated, highly organized, have good communication skills, and be able to work in a team environment. Digital imaging projects require not just knowledge of digitization, but the ability to identify condition problems in the originals, a basic understanding of the techniques used to create the originals being digitized (e.g., an understanding of photographic techniques), knowledge of the historical significance of the originals, cataloging skills, database design and management skills, web design skills, and possibly graphic design skills as well. If your existing staff or the temporary staff you intend to hire for the project do not have these skills, be sure to include time and money for training in your budget and time line. Many projects utilize existing staff. Will they be expected to continue their normal work duties for the duration of the project? In many cases, the answer is yes, so remember that when defining your time line. Consider working with volunteers and student interns to help save on staffing costs.

Suggested Staffing Needs

Project director. Oversees project; maintains budget, time line, overall work flow

Collections assessor. Selects originals, checks condition and makes recommendations for treatment, rehouses originals as needed, and reshelves originals once digitization and cataloging are complete

Database technician. Creates and maintains any necessary databases for the project, including but not limited to the metadata database

Scanning technician. Handles original objects, creates scans, creates all necessary surrogates, records all digital image metadata, and creates backup files on the chosen storage media. Note: The scanning technician will check the image files against the project benchmarks; however, it is highly recommended that another staff member actually perform quality control on the image files.

Quality control technician. Checks image files generated by the scanning technician against the project benchmarks and records any additional digital image metadata

Cataloger. Creates all catalog records or edits existing records for digital images of originals included in the project. Note: As with quality control of the digital image files, it is a good idea to have another staff member check the catalog records as well. This can be as simple as a grammar check or a detailed check for accuracy of subject headings.

Web technician. If you project includes the creation of a web access component and you are creating that portion of the project in-house, you will need a web technician who can design and maintain your website.[1]

DEFINING A TIME LINE

Defining a time line can be one of the most tedious aspects of preparing for a digital imaging project, but it is vital to achieving your goals. A time line will force you to have a better understanding of every step of a digital project before you begin. You may not stick to the time line once the project begins, but it gives you a place to start and a sense for what must be accomplished. Here are several things to consider when defining your time line:

Object preparation. This is entirely dependent on the condition of the originals. If your project involves collection material that is fragile or will need conservation treatment prior to scanning, be sure to give yourself plenty of time for object preparation. Glass plate negatives, for example, often need to be cleaned before they are scanned. You must consider the time implications of cleaning each plate. If your project includes documents that are extremely fragile, moving them on and off the scanner will be a slow process, which will greatly impact the number of scans generated each day. The act of simply pulling the originals and organizing them in a way that makes digitization as efficient as possible will take time.

Conservation treatment. If any of your objects need conservation treatment prior to digitization, the delay could mean months. Conservation treatment is often quite time-consuming, depending on what needs to be done. Another time factor will be transportation to and from the treatment location if you do not have a conservator on site. Because this can have such an impact on a digital project, be sure to know well in advance of the start of your project what items will need treatment prior to digitization. This will help you budget accordingly as well.

Scans per day. Calculate the number of scans you will generate each day. If you do not already own a scanner, talk to people who use similar equipment to make your estimation. Base your calculations on the speed of the scanner, the resolution of the master image files, the efficiency of your scanning technicians, the speed of your local area network (if applicable), the speed of your computer processor, and the speed of your CD burner (if applicable).

Web-ready image files. How many surrogate files can be generated per day? This will be dependent on your computer processor speeds, the amount of random access memory (RAM) in your computer, and whether you utilize batching software. Some image manipulation software packages offer batching procedures that allow you to tell the computer to open every file in a particular folder, run a series of alterations to those files automatically (e.g., changing the resolution), and save them in another location. Using batching tools greatly speeds up the creation of surrogate image files.

Quality control of image files. Be sure to include time for quality control of the image files. You may discover that once your scanning technician is reaching the benchmarks on the files, you will no longer need to check every file. In reality, you may not have time to check every file. If this is the case, determine an appropriate percentage to check. There is no consensus from project to project what is an adequate percentage. It is entirely dependent on the size of your project and the skill of your scanning technician. Be sure to include time for a certain percentage of redos—image files that do not meet the benchmarks and must be rescanned.

Cataloging. The time it takes to catalog an item will depend on whether any previous cataloging exists, how detailed the information is within the item, what is known about the item, and how detailed your want your catalog records to be. The more knowledgeable your cataloger is with cataloging procedures, the quicker the cataloging will be accomplished. For example, is your cataloger familiar with using thesauri, and has he or she worked with the collection materials before?

Quality control of catalog records. It is a good idea to have someone check your catalog records much as you perform quality control on the image files. This is time-consuming so you may consider spot-checking the records or checking certain portions of the records, such as the subject element, to make sure the subject headings are entered correctly.

Online access tools. Will you have to learn how to build the online access portion of your project, or will you hire someone to do this for you? In either case, you need to include time for beta testing the online component before the end of the project. Consider a regular schedule of uploading as you finish surrogate files and catalog records.

Be sure to leave yourself plenty of time for the scanning learning curve, redoing scans if they do not pass quality control, and fixing problems discovered during the beta testing of the online component. Things always happen during a digital project to slow the schedule. Give yourself time to get into a good work flow, and include time at the end of the project for unexpected events.

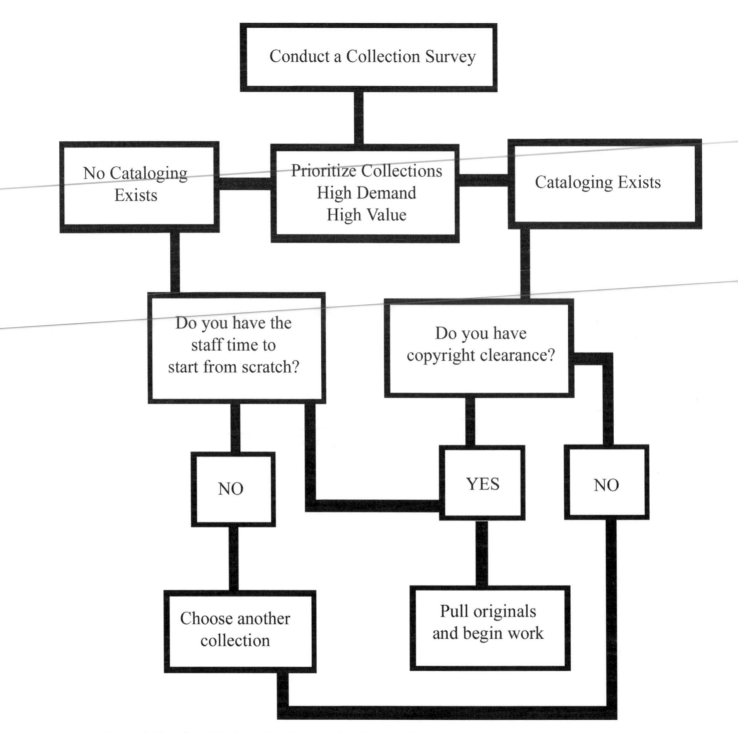

Figure 4.1 Work Flow for Digital Imaging Project: Choosing a Collection.

WORK FLOW

Efficient work flow is key to the success of any digital imaging project. Figures 4.1 and 4.2 are two charts designed to help you visualize work flow within your project. The first is a brief outline to help you determine if a collection is the right one for your project.

The second will take you through the process of creating digital image files and metadata.

MAKING YOUR GRANT COMPETITIVE

Finding an agency to fund digital imaging projects is not difficult. Making your grant competitive is. Federal

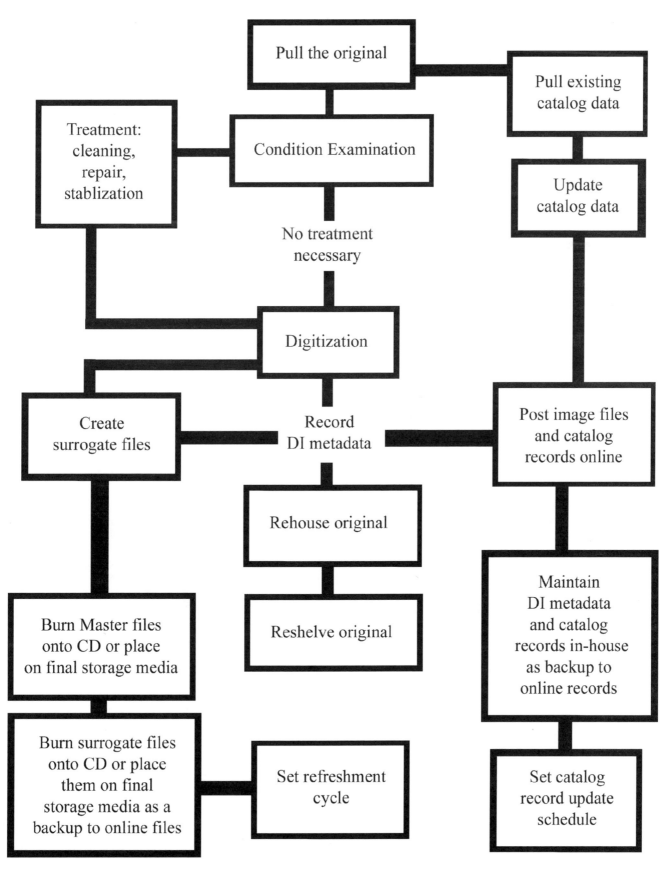

Figure 4.2   Work Flow for Digital Imaging Project: Creating the Final Product.

grant funding sources for digital imaging projects include the National Endowment for the Humanities (NEH), the Institute of Museum and Library Services (IMLS), and the National Endowment for the Arts (NEA). State funding sources for digital imaging projects include state humanities councils and state library commissions. Local private foundations and private individuals should not be overlooked as a source of funding for your project. Many times these resources are not fully tapped and the competition not as steep.

A good grant proposal will have more than enough matching funds, include a well-defined budget and time line, show that the staff and institution have a good understanding and proven knowledge of the technology, and outline the need for better access to the original materials chosen for the project. As with most grants, the more matching funds your institution can provide, the better. Consider using the costs for rehousing materials as matching funds. If you utilize existing staff, their salaries will be matched. If you can find alternative funding sources for the digitization equipment, that can be used as match. Next, be incredibly specific about your benchmarks. Digital imaging grant proposals are very popular, and the reviewers are quite digitally savvy, so they look for pointers in the proposal that show the project staff truly understand digital imaging and its implications. Clearly defined benchmarks that include a discussion about your refreshment procedures, even if you will not start refreshment until several years after the completion of the project, will go a long way toward convincing a grant reviewer you know what you are talking about. Be very clear when describing your delivery system. If possible, build and mount a prototype you can point reviewers to when they get your proposal. This will help prove your knowledge of web-based access to cultural materials.

CONCLUSION

Creating a healthy budget and a realistic time line will not only help you when applying for those extremely competitive digital imaging grants but will also prove to your administration, your board, and your staff that you are ready for the digital arena. Digital imaging projects are complex, but with the right planning and reasonable goals, your project will succeed.

NOTE

1. This information and more suggestions on staffing needs are available in the Digital Imaging Best Practices Version 1.0, Western Trails Digital Standards Group, January 2003, available on the Colorado Digitization Program website at http://www.cdpheritage.org/westerntrails/wt_bpscanning.html

CHAPTER 5

Technical Specifications: Establishing Benchmarks

BENCHMARKS ARE TECHNICAL SPECIFICATIONS ESTAB-lished in order to obtain the best possible digital representation of the original. They are a vital step in any digital project regardless of the objects being digitized. Benchmarks are also important because they play a role in quality control. There are currently no national standards for digital imaging benchmarks, only best practices. It is unlikely that national standards recognized and adopted by the American National Standards Institute (ANSI) will emerge until the evolution of digital technology stabilizes. As this technology evolves, so must digital benchmarks.

It is a good idea to establish a set of basic benchmarks before purchasing equipment, as this will help in the selection process. Once your equipment is installed and operating, it may be necessary to tweak the benchmarks to fit the specifications of your scanner. Hopefully this will mean improving them rather than dropping back on your requirements. Benchmarks include, but are not limited to, specifications for spatial resolution, file format, and color requirements. Without a set of predefined benchmarks, quality control on files generated in-house or through an outsourcing vendor will be virtually impossible.

SPATIAL RESOLUTION

To create benchmarks that will work for your project, several technical questions need to be answered. First, at what resolution are you going to scan? Deciding on a resolution is entirely dependent on the size of the originals and the use to which you plan to put the files. In chapter 2, we discussed whether your digital project was for preservation or access. If your project is designed to create image files from your collection that will be compatible for use in a variety of ways, your resolution benchmarks must be considerably higher than if your intent is only to create image files for the Internet. Keep in mind, as stressed in chapter 2, that the cost of digital imaging projects in dollars as well as staff time and resources is high, making projects designed strictly

as access tools on the Internet no longer feasible. If your institution is making the commitment to digital technology, follow the rule "Scan once; scan right; scan for the future," and create master image files at the highest resolution you can afford.

Determining resolution benchmarks will require a bit of testing once your equipment is in place. Current best practices suggest for master image files a minimum of 600 pixels per inch (ppi) for text-based originals or 3,000 to 5,000 ppi on the long dimension for photographic originals.[1] First, determine the highest optical resolution your scanner can capture. Then pull out representative size examples from your collection to be digitized and run some resolution tests. The point of this exercise is to determine the best resolution for each size represented by your original objects. The best resolution will depend not only on the size of the object but on the condition as well. For example, if your project involves digitizing handwritten manuscripts, at what resolution will the smallest part of the text in your document be legible? If the ink or pencil is difficult to read on the original, a higher resolution may be required. Ultimately, you want to generate the highest-resolution file you can afford. This will ensure you only scan the object once. At the Nebraska State Historical Society (NSHS), the minimum resolution is 800 ppi for an 8 × 10 original. The resolution jumps to a minimum of 3,000 ppi for a 35mm slide. The Denver Public Library (DPL) looks first at the pixel dimension, rather than a resolution of so many pixels per inch. For example, to achieve a high-quality digital version of an 8 × 10 black-and-white photograph, DPL generates a file that is 5,000 pixels on the long dimension. To achieve 5,000 pixels on the ten-inch side of a photograph, all that is necessary is a resolution of 300 ppi. The difference between these two techniques results in substantially different file sizes, but neither technique is better than the other; they are simply different ways of approaching the same result, which is to create a high-quality image file that will suit the needs of the digital project.

Table 5.1 Possible Resolutions for Master Image File Capture

Size of Original	File Resolution	Pixel Dimension	File Size RGB	File Size Grayscale
1 × 2 inches	5500 ppi	5600 × 11200	180MB	60MB
2 × 3 inches	3000 ppi	6000 × 9000	155MB	52MB
4 × 5 inches	2400 ppi	9600 × 12000	330MB	110MB
5 × 7 inches	1200 ppi	6000 × 8400	144MB	48MB
8 × 10 inches	800 ppi	6400 × 8000	146MB	48MB
11 × 14 inches	800 ppi	8800 × 11200	282MB	94MB

Table 5.1 is a chart listing possible resolutions for master image file capture based on original object size created for use at the NSHS digital imaging laboratory. These resolutions are *only suggestions* and are substantially higher than those recommended by best practices guidelines.[2]

It is vital that you run your own tests before finalizing resolution benchmarks. Think carefully about the potential uses of your image files. Think also about hard copy prints. How large are the prints you generate for your patrons or for exhibitions? Will the resolution you choose be enough to enlarge a 2 × 3 inch original to an 8 × 10 print for a researcher or an 8 × 10 original to a 20 × 24 inch print for exhibition? The larger the print size, the more information you need, so the higher the necessary resolution. Will your image files be used for publication? If so, what resolution is needed by the publisher? The answers to these questions as well as testing the scanner against your collection will help you determine the best resolutions for your master file benchmarks.

Figures 5.1 and 5.2 illustrate how resolution affects the amount of information captured in the image file.

Figure 5.1 NSHS RG2608.PH-1764.

| 150 ppi | 300 ppi | 600 ppi | 800 ppi | 1200 ppi | 2400 ppi | 3175 ppi |

Figure 5.2   Close-up of NSHS RG2608.PH-1764.

This is a glass plate negative measuring 6 × 8 inches. The arrow points to a portion of the image approximately ¼ inch in size. As shown in figure 5.2, close examination of this small part of the photograph shows extreme differences in detail from 150 ppi to 3,175 ppi. Note: At 3,175 ppi, this 6 × 8 inch glass plate negative, scanned in grayscale, produces a 618-megabyte (MB) file.

As you increase the optical resolution on your scanner, you will eventually reach what is termed the *resolution threshold*. This is the point where no matter how many more pixels you add per inch, you are no longer gaining information from the original. At some point, depending on the size of the object, the visual information captured from the original can become obscured by the structural components of the object itself. When files are viewed at 100 percent or 1:1, paper fiber can interfere with reading the text of a manuscript, and cracks in the emulsion of photographic prints will make seeing small details in the image more difficult. Just as there is no one resolution perfect for every object, there is no one resolution threshold. Determining when the resolution is too high must be based on personal experience. But remember, just because your scanner can capture at high optical resolutions does not mean it is appropriate to do so. Capturing at extremely high resolutions, such as 3,000 ppi for an 8 × 10 original, is very time-consuming and will drastically slow down your work flow. However, the benefits can be enormous. Try to determine what resolution best fits your collection and your needs. Expect that your resolution benchmark for the master image file will vary based on object size.

Resolution for surrogate files also depends on their intended use. Many cultural institutions are not mount-ing web-based images at higher than 150 ppi. This enables use online but prohibits good reproduction quality when downloaded for print purposes. Mounting low-resolution files helps institutions protect their collections. In some cases, higher-resolution images are available online, but the pixel dimension is altered to achieve the same goal. To determine surrogate image resolutions, create a chart that lists the types of uses these files will see and compare it to the list of suggested resolutions in table 5.2. Again, these are just suggestions, not national standards.

Table 5.2   Determining Surrogate Image Resolutions

Type of Use	Resolution / Pixel Dimension[1]
Websites	72–300 ppi/600–3000 pixels long
Low-end publication (brochures)	150–400 ppi
Prints for researchers	200–300 ppi, depending on printer
Prints for exhibition	300 ppi[2]
High-end publication (coffee table book)	800 ppi

1. Pixel dimension always refers to the long side of the object, regardless of vertical or horizontal position.
2. Large format prints will not require high resolution, but will require larger pixel dimensions to cover the size of the final print. Generally, the simplest solution is to take a master file, preferably one generated at higher than 600 ppi, change the pixel dimension to cover the final print size (it may be necessary to change the measuring tool to inches for this step) and then drop the resolution to 300 ppi file, which is suitable for most printers.

FILE FORMATS

Master image files should always be created and stored as tiff files. A *tiff file* is an uncompressed file format and therefore is not decreased in size when the file is saved. This makes the file much more stable for long-term use since there is no chance of information loss due to compression or corruption of the compression algorithm. Surrogate files are often compressed as lossless jpegs. This makes the file much smaller so it requires less storage space, is quicker to upload on web pages, and results in faster download times for researchers.

COLOR SPACE

Should a digital file be generated in RGB or grayscale? The answer lies with the original object and whether any color information that exists is important for end users of the digital image. Remember, one major point of a digital project is to scan the object only once. If color exists and is not captured, you may regret the decision in the future. If your goal in digitization is to provide researchers with the best representation of the original, then color is important, even if it is only a letter written using red ink. Without the color, the digital representation takes on a different meaning. Think carefully before deciding to eliminate color.

Color is not just about capturing your original object in RGB; it is also about bit depth (see table 5.3). The higher the bit depth, the more color information is captured per pixel. Grayscale images are captured in 8 bits, which contain 256 shades of gray or 16 bits, containing over 65,000 shades of gray. RGB files, captured in 24 bits, contain 16 million colors; 48 bits captures over 281 trillion colors. Capturing in higher bit depths increases your ability to accurately represent the original, but it also dramatically increases file size. Another point to keep in mind is that most computer screens only display in 24 bits, and most image manipulations software is only capable of limited functionality with files captured in higher than 32-bit RGB. Computer monitors and software will continue to evolve and improve, so if you scanner can capture at 48 bits and the file sizes remain manageable, utilize that higher bit depth for your master image file. You can always drop down in bit depth on your surrogate files.

HOW TO ACHIEVE IMAGE FILES THAT PASS QUALITY CONTROL

What constitutes a good scan? Aside from meeting your benchmarks, a good scan is judged by using a histogram. It is not enough to open the master file, look at it on your computer screen, and say, "Yeah, that looks good." Quality control checks using histograms make the process of judging image quality less subjective.

A histogram is a graphic representation of the tonal value in an image file. Each pixel in an image file is assigned a numeric value between 0 and 255; 0 is the blackest black, and 255 is the whitest white. Figure 5.3 shows a histogram generated using Adobe Photoshop® 7.0. Once a histogram is generated, it allows you to check the whitest white and blackest black to ensure no details where lost during the scan. By providing a graphic representation of the image, you can more accurately check for loss of detail. To read the histogram, move your mouse over the graph. Numbers between 0 and 255 will appear next to the word *Level* at the top of the second column below the histogram.

No master image file should contain pixels with values lower than 9 or higher than 247.[3] Values lower than 9 will create areas of the image that are so black they contain no detail. Value higher than 247 will be so white they, too, will contain no detail and no ink will be used in those areas when making a print, so the parts of the image higher than 247 will be paper-white. If scanner software is allowed to remain on automatic, the default settings will look for the lightest area of the original and assign it a numeric value of 255. Likewise, the darkest area will be assigned 0. This obliterates any information in the highlights and shadow areas. Taking the software off automatic to set the white and black points at the time of image capture is a vital part of creating a master file that contains good detail in both highlight and shadow areas.

Table 5.3 Color as Determined by Bit Depth

	Nebraska State Historical Society Benchmarks		
File Type	Resolution	Color/Bit Depth	File Format
Master	See chart on page 3	48 bit RGB/16 bit Grayscale	tif
Print	300 ppi	32 bit RGB/8 bit Grayscale	tif
Reference	150 ppi/600 pixels[1]	32 bit RGB/8 bit Grayscale	jpg
Thumbnail	72 ppi	32 bit RGB/8 bit Grayscale	jpg

1. The reference file is set at 600 pixels on the long dimension.

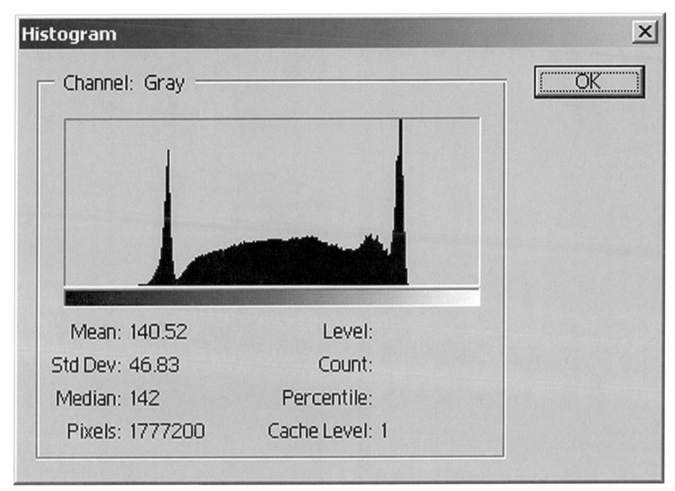

Figure 5.3 Histogram.

Control is everything when it comes to scanning software. It is important to be able to set the output points in the scanning software in order to stop the scanner from assigning the brightest point 255 and darkest point 0. Look for output levels in the preferences or options menus of your software. Another place to try is within the shadow and highlight control panels, if they exist. Often times there will be places to set input levels, but you need the output levels. It does not matter whether you set input levels at 9 and 247; once the file is transferred out of the scanner software, those levels will be changed to 0 and 255. Call the scanner technicians if you have trouble locating this vital tool. It may be hidden in an obscure location because so few users care about this setting. If your scanner software does not allow you this type of control, buy new software or a new scanner.

Compare figure 5.4, a cabinet card, circa 1900, scanned using automatic settings, with figure 5.5, the same photograph scanned using a white point output level of 247 and a black point output level of 9. Figure

5.4 looks fine; it is bright, punchy, and clear. In fact, it looks like a new photograph. Figure 5.5, however, is a much closer representation of the original. Obviously you will have to take my word for that, since I cannot include the original in this text. However, look closely at the white areas of these two files. Notice how much detail is lost in figure 5.4, the file generated on automatic and therefore having a white point of 255. Just because an image file looks okay does not mean it is okay.

Figures 5.6 and 5.7 are the histograms for figures 5.4 and 5.5. Notice the difference in range from black to white. Figure 5.6 shows pixels spread across the entire range from 0 to 255. This is a direct result of using automatic settings in the scanning software. The scanner determines the brightest area in the photograph and assigns that area a value of 255. It does a similar thing with the blackest area by assigning those areas a value of 0. In figure 5.6, there are 224 pixels with a value of 255 (see the level and count numbers below the his-

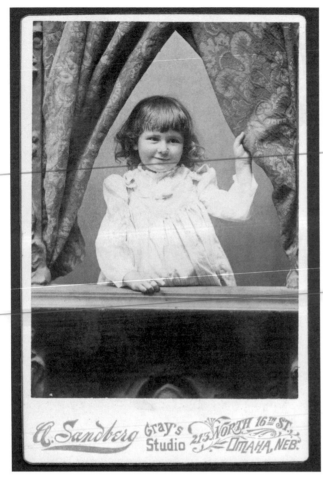

Figure 5.4 NSHS Archives Photograph Teaching Collections.

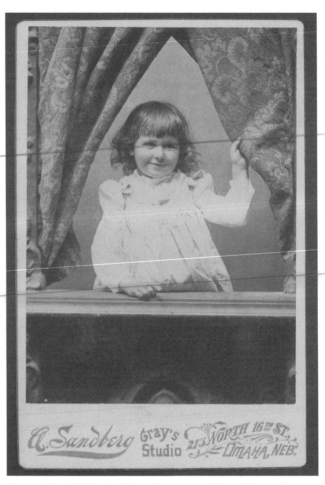

Figure 5.5 NSHS Archives Photograph Teaching Collections.

togram graph). Figure 5.7 shows the brightest white in the image, only two pixels, having a value of 219. Although the scan itself looks flat and dull, it is a much closer representation of the original. Remember, you

can always adjust the contrast to increase the white and black tones to make the image look better for printing and website use. It is vital, however, to create a master scan that accurately represents the original.

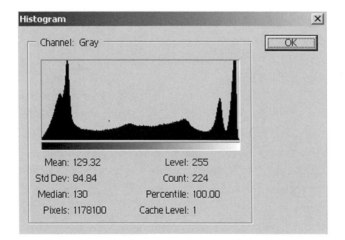

Figure 5.6   Histogram with Black and White Levels outside Appropriate Benchmarks.

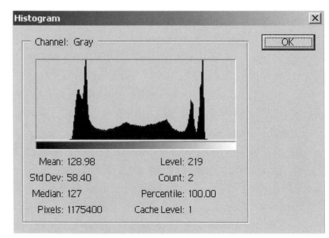

Figure 5.7   Histogram with Black and White Levels within Appropriate Benchmarks.

CLIPPING, SPIKING, AND GAPS IN HISTOGRAMS

Clipping, spiking, and gaps are important characteristics to look for and avoid in histograms. Clipping results from the incorrect setup of white and black points in the scanning software. If white and black are improperly set, everything above or below those points is "clipped" or registers as the same tone. When clipping occurs, the scanning operator has misjudged the actual white or black points in the image and must re-scan the original using different settings for the white or black point. Some scanning software indicates where the white and black points are located within the preview of the original. However, this feature is available only on very high-end scanners. Most software will show a window that gives the numeric value of the pixels in the image as you pass the cursor over the preview. This makes it easier to determine where the white and black points are in the image.

Spiking on the ends of the histogram usually indicates clipping. This problem also shows up in the image itself as blockage and pixelization in the shadows and blowouts in the highlights. Acceptable spikes can occur if a large portion of the original object contains one color value—for example, if a black and white photograph has a gray sky with no detail or a broadside contains large areas of background that are the same color. Be aware of the color values in your original objects. This will help you determine whether a spike in the histogram cannot be avoided.

Gaps in histograms result from too much contrast adjustment. This can happen at the time of capture if changes to the histogram or tonal range are made in the scanning software. It can also happen when contrast is adjusted in image manipulation software. Gaps in the histogram are not acceptable in master image files; however, they may be unavoidable in surrogate files that must be adjusted for printing or web delivery. Extreme gaps will be obvious without opening the histogram because the image file will not look good on screen.

Figure 5.8 shows a good histogram created from the image file in figure 5.9 with no gaps or clipping. There are some spikes toward both ends of the histogram, but they represent the large number of pixels for a particular tonal value and are not a problem. Spikes are only a problem if they appear at the extreme ends of the histogram and represent clipping.

Figure 5.10 represents the image file in figure 5.11. It has undergone contrast adjustment resulting in gaps within the histogram and an inaccurate representation of the original. The file may look more pleasing, but it will not pass quality control checks. This is only inappropriate if the histogram is from a master image file. Many surrogate files adjusted for print or website use will have gaps in their histograms.

Figure 5.12 shows spikes and clipping on the ends of the histogram caused by extreme contrast adjustment to the image in figure 5.13. Note the count of pixels, 181,964 at the level 0, or the blackest black in the image. This indicates clipping or the incorrect setting of black points during the scan. You can also see gaps in the histogram caused by the scanning software forcing the tonal range across the entire spread of 0 and 255.

DEALING WITH COLOR

Color can be a problem in digital imaging projects. Because scanners, printers, and computer monitors all interpret color differently, every piece of digital capture equipment has the potential to record color differently. Purple ink on an original document may look purple when scanned by one scanner, but it might look more like blue when digitized on another scanner. Computer monitors display color differently, too. A color image opened on one computer will look very different on another, even if the monitors are from the same manufacturer.

So how do you know when the color is accurate? As a user on the Internet, you never know. As the creator of the image file, you have several options. One is to use color calibration software. This software makes your scanner, monitor, and printer see color in the same way, thereby enabling accurate color representation at all three stations.[4] Color calibration will not, however, solve the problem of accurate color display once the image file is online and users around the world are viewing the image on a plethora of monitors. Color calibration software is very expensive, has a steep learning curve, requires constant adjustments, and only benefits your ability to accurately display color on in-house hardware that is part of the calibration system. The primary users of this software are printing companies and other graphics firms.

The solution in use by some libraries, museums, and

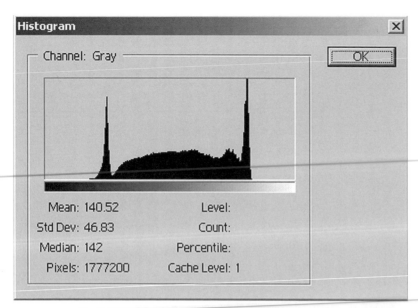

Figure 5.8 A Histogram of a Good Digital Image.

Figure 5.9 NSHS RG0716.PH:31-11.

archives is to scan a color bar along with the original object. Color bars come from the photograph print world. Companies that process and print film use color bars to calibrate their printing machines. The use of standardized color bars makes the color on your latest snapshots accurate. Including a color bar in your image file enables any user to adjust their monitor in order for the image file to be accurately displayed.

Several different companies manufacture a variety of color bars, including Eastman Kodak and Nuritsu. Most color bars do not include every color, so the use of color bars is at best a stopgap solution. An image file including a color bar will not display accurately on monitors unless the user knows how the color bar should look and knows how to adjust the monitor for accurate viewing. At best, including a color bar gives the image file a standardized reference point from which to begin. Note: Including a color bar in your image files, master or surrogates, will increase the scan time and the file size.

STORAGE MEDIA

Several types of storage media are currently available for digital image files. The two most commonly used are CDRs and local area networks (LANs). When storing image files on CDRs, be sure to set the CD writer to create an ISO9660 CDR. Current best practices recognize ISO9660 as the appropriate format for CDRs.[5] Making an ISO9660 CD will make the CD compatible with any CD drive, regardless of age. CD-RWs, or rewritable CDs, are becoming popular but are not compatible with older CD drives, which might cause problems if you plan to loan your CDs. The best bet for ease of retrievability of image files, and to ensure no problems with drives that find CD-RWs tricky, is to stick with an ISO9660 CDR.

A CDR officially holds 650 MB of data.

In reality, it is closer to 645 MB. When deciding which storage media to use consider this: At the end of your project, how many CDs will be created, where will they be stored, and how will you track which image file is on which CD? If using CDs, it is best to generate two sets, one for use and the other stored off-site, preferably in a different building, as a backup. CDs are extremely cheap, especially when purchased in bulk, but they require shelf space, location data to track image file locations, and, most importantly, refreshment.

Refreshment is the transfer of data from one media to another before that media deteriorates or becomes obsolete. Have you noticed that most new computers now come with DVD drives, rather than CD drives? Computer technology changes quickly, and it is vital to refresh your image files regularly to ensure retrievability of the data.

Some CD manufacturers claim their product will last one hundred years or more. That is irrelevant. No computer will exist in one hundred years with a CD drive. So even if your CDs are still intact, which is debatable, you will have no way to retrieve your files. Refreshment is the answer. Refreshment cycles should begin three to five years after the creation of the image file and its subsequent burning to CD. The CDs are checked and the files transferred to new CDs or whatever new media best suits your institution's needs. Refreshment cycles should not be longer than five years, especially if your CDs are seeing extensive use.

Local area networks can provide storage for master files and surrogate files while at the same time offering backups to tape drives or mirrored hard drives. A properly backed-up LAN system allows for few worries about loss of data or problems with data access due to CD deterioration or lack of refreshment. It also eliminates the need for valuable shelf space to store CDs, whose

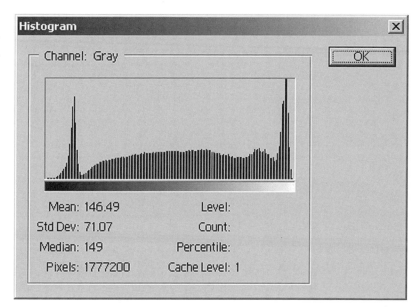

Figure 5.10 A Histogram with Gaps.

Figure 5.11 NSHS RG0716.PH:31-11.

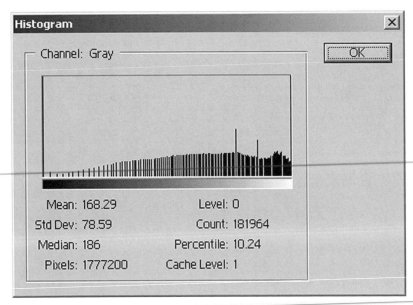

Figure 5.12 **Spikes and Clipping on the Ends of the Histogram.**

numbers can quickly climb into the thousands. The only limitation to a LAN system is the amount of storage space available although many systems can now hold terabytes of data.[6] The more storage space on a LAN, the more expensive it becomes. Another advantage to a LAN system is the staff time saved from not having to track image file locations on CDs and then retrieve those CDs in order to access the files.

Digital versatile disks (DVDs) are the newest storage solution technology. At this time, museums, libraries, and archives are just beginning to use DVDs to store digitized film, video, and audio, rather than still images of collection materials. DVD technology is still in its infancy. There are several types of DVDs: DVD-R, DVD+R, and DVD±R. None of the best practices guidelines recommend using this media for data storage. Eventually as the technology evolves, CDRs and CD-RWs will be completely replaced by DVD or some other new technology, but in the meantime, if LAN systems are not feasible for your budget, choose CDs rather than DVDs.

CONCLUSION

Understanding technical specifications and establishing benchmarks will go a long way toward making your digital imaging efforts successful. These seemingly small details are the core of any digital project. Making good choices here will prove beneficial as technology continues to evolve.

NOTES

1. *Digital Imaging Best Practices Version 1.0*, Western Trails Digital Standards Group, January 2003, p. 26; available online at www.cdpheritage.org/westerntrails/wt_bpscanning.html.

Figure 5.13 **NSHS RG0716.PH:31-11.**

2. *Digital Imaging Best Practices Version 1.0*, Western Trails Digital Standards Group, January 2003; available online at www.cdpheritage.org/westerntrails/wt_bpscanning.html.

3. These values are based on standards set by the Nebraska State Historical Society in 1998.

4. For more information on color calibration, see Franzeska Frey's *Guides to Quality in Visual Resource Imaging, 5: File Formats for Digital Masters*, produced for the Digital Library Federation and the Resource Library Group and available online at www.rlg.org/visguides/index.html.

5. *Digital Imaging Best Practices Version 1.0*, Western Trails Digital Standards Group, January 2003; available online at www.cdpheritage.org/westerntrails/wt_bpscanning.html.

6. A megabyte equals just over one million bytes, a gigabyte equals just over one billion bytes, and a terabyte equals just over one trillion bytes.

CHAPTER 6

Choosing Equipment

CHOOSING DIGITIZATION EQUIPMENT CAN BE A LOT OF fun but at the same time very confusing. Digital imaging equipment comes in many shapes, sizes, capabilities, and features. Keep in mind when choosing equipment that digital projects have a tremendous impact on the collections being digitized. Make sure you purchase equipment that will not harm the objects while they are being scanned. This may seem like an obvious point, but damage can occur easily to precious originals. Make sure the scanner is not the cause. Talk to other people who use the equipment you are considering. Even if they do not have the same scanner, there is a good chance the scanning software will be the same within a manufacturer's line of products. Find out whether they like the equipment and software. Try to see some of the files they have created so you can compare them to your benchmarks.

The first question you need to answer is, What you are going to scan? Does your project include three-dimensional objects, oversize maps or broadsides, bound materials such as ledger books or journals, paintings, photographic prints, or negatives? The type of material you include in your digital project will determine what type of digital capture equipment you need to purchase. Flat objects, such as photographic prints, letters, and even relatively flat coins or buttons, can be scanned on most typical flatbed scanners. Negatives or transparencies that require transmitted light need a special feature called a *transparency adapter* in order to digitize using a flatbed scanner. Three-dimensional objects, such as sculpture, furniture, or clothing, cannot be digitized using a scanner. If your project includes such items, you will need a digital camera or photographic copies of the objects.

What size are the originals? If your project involves 35mm slides or strips of 35mm film, you may decide to purchase a scanner designed strictly for that media. These scanners provide high-quality reproduction of small-format slides and negatives and, depending on the model, can be purchased for between $700 and $2,000. Size is very important because the smaller the

original, the higher the optical resolution you will need to capture enough information to make your digital files usable.[1]

If you are scanning manuscripts, are they typescripts or handwritten? How small is the text? The smaller the text, the higher the resolution necessary to capture the information, and this will make the scanner more expensive. When scanning from text-based materials, be sure to consider whether you want the end result to be a digital image of each page or text-searchable files. Text-searchable files require optical character recognition (OCR) software. This software creates a text document, like a Microsoft Word file, rather than a digital image file, like a tiff image. These formats are mutually exclusive and require different types of software to generate.

If you are hoping to digitize large objects such as maps or broadsides you may run into trouble trying to do this on a typical flatbed scanner. Most flatbed scanners have a scanning area, also called the *bed size*, no greater than 12 × 17 inches. For very large flat objects, you will need a digital camera or high-quality photographic copies that can be digitized on a scanner. Note: Most digital cameras are not suitable for digitization projects because they capture image files as compressed jpegs, and the file sizes and resolutions are too small for long-term file viability.[2]

The second question is, How much money do you have to spend on digitization equipment? You will need money not only for a scanner but for a computer as well. Buy a computer with the fastest processor and as much RAM as you can afford. The faster the computer's processor and the more RAM you have, the faster your image processing will go. More RAM will also allow you to have multiple programs running so you can catalog your images as you run processing or as the scans are being generated.

When buying a computer, also consider the size of the monitor. Buy a computer with the largest monitor you can afford. The larger the monitor, the easier it will be for you to evaluate the image files—after all, that is what digital imaging projects are all about.

Finally, when it comes to equipment, as with most things in life, you get what you pay for! If you are lucky and have plenty of money to spend on equipment, put a majority of your funds into the capture equipment rather than the computer. The better the capture tool, the better your image files.

PICKING A SCANNER

Not only do you need to choose the right scanner based on what type of materials you are digitizing; you also need to pay close attention to the scanning software. Control is everything. You must be able to adjust the software manually; in other words, you have to be able to take it off automatic. Talk to the vendor or manufacturer about white and black points. Find out whether you can set those points, rather than relying on the scanning software to do it for you. If you cannot adjust the white and black points individually for each scan, can you adjust the output levels? Check to see whether the scanner has automatic sharpening and whether it is possible to turn that off. This control will greatly increase your ability to accurately capture the original.[3] If the vendor or manufacturer's representative does not know what you are talking about, ask to talk to a technician at the company or pick a different manufacturer.

Optical resolution is also important. Do not buy a scanner that has an optical resolution lower than 600 ppi, which is the minimum at which you should digitize. Many scanner manufacturers tout their equipment as having resolutions over 36,000 ppi. This is *interpolated resolution*, meaning the computer adds data rather than actually capturing it off the object, and this point is irrelevant to your project. Remember to keep in mind the size of the materials you are digitizing when comparing optical resolution. The smaller your original, the higher the resolution needed. The higher the optical resolution of the scanner, the more expensive it will be. Buy a scanner with the highest optical resolution you can afford.

Dynamic range is another vital specification to consider. The greater the dynamic range, the more tonal values the scanner can recognize. And of course, the greater the dynamic range, the more expensive the scan-

ner. Many scanners have a dynamic range between 3.2 and 3.7. The best scanners coming on the market have dynamic ranges over 4.0. High dynamic ranges are particularly important for photographic media. Even if your project does not initially involve photographs, dynamic range will affect the image file results. Buy a scanner with the highest dynamic range you can afford.

Size of the scanner bed will affect the size of the original you can capture and, of course, the cost of the scanner. The larger the scanner bed, the larger the original you can scan. You will want to leave at least a quarter of an inch around the original during capture, so take that into consideration when judging bed sizes. You may also want to include a color bar when scanning in RGB, so think of that when comparing bed sizes as well. Most flatbed scanners offer bed sizes between 8 × 12 inches and 12 × 17 inches. Even if your current digital project only includes originals that are 8 × 10 inches, consider buying a scanner with a larger bed for future projects. If you invest now in a high-end scanner that offers more than your current project requires, your future digitization efforts will be more flexible.

Scanner speed directly affects the work flow and time line of your project. Find out how long it takes the scanner to generate a digital image file. Caution: Although this information is usually available in the technical specifications, beware, because it is often presented as the speed at which the scanner generates a file at a low resolution, not necessarily the speed of the scanner at the resolution you have chosen for your benchmarks. As a general rule, the higher the resolution, the longer it takes the scanner to generate a file. For example, a scanning technician using a Creo Eversmart Pro® scanner, digitizing 8 × 10 inch original objects at 800 ppi, can generate approximately thirty-five scans during an eight-hour work day. To digitize an 8 × 10 original at 3,175 ppi, the scanner's highest optical resolution, takes forty-five minutes for a single scan. The specifications from the manufacturer list the scan times at forty-five scans per hour based on 6 × 7 centimeter originals scanned at 250 percent of original size at 300 ppi. Forty-five scans an hour sounds fast, but the file specifications used to create those scans are nowhere near the benchmarks for the creation of master image files. Find someone who has a scanner similar to the one you are considering, and ask how many scans they can generate in an hour using your benchmarks.

If your project includes transmitted light materials, you will need a scanner with a transparency adapter. Sometimes these are large, heavy lids that replace the standard lid. On other models, the scanner has a drawer underneath the CCD and light source.[4] Either design has its good and bad points. Adapters as lids can create problems when scanning fragile objects. The heavier lid will put more pressure on the original and may cause damage. Trays that slide in and out under the CCD are often stiff and require extra care once the originals are in place. Many times the film holders used in the tray do not leave extra space around the edge of the negative. Depending on the type of negative, this can cause problems when trying to capture the entire sheet of film, particularly with holders designed for 4 × 5 or 35mm negatives. Some scanners that utilize trays for transparent materials offer a generic holder that covers the entire capture area. This holder can work for glass plate negatives or any size film, but the movement of the drawer can cause the materials to move out of alignment and even overlap. Some attempts to overcome this problem include placing an additional piece of glass over the originals in the drawer, but this approach is dangerous, especially if those originals are fragile. It also introduces another layer between the original and the CCD. If the glass used to keep the originals in place is not perfect, those defects will affect the quality of the scan. Low-cost transparency adapters give marginal results depending on the type of materials being digitized. Ask the manufacturer whether you can run a series of tests with the equipment before purchasing if you are unable to find someone with a similar scanner who will help you run preliminary tests.

As with any computer equipment, the minute you buy a scanner, a newer and better one will come on the market. Don't let this be a factor in your decision. Choose a scanner that meets your needs, and spend as much money as you can afford. Buy a scanner with software that gives you complete control; get the highest optical resolution, the greatest dynamic range, and the largest scanner bed you can afford. Remember, this scanner will not last forever, but it needs to give you immediate results that will meet your benchmarks.

DIGITAL CAMERAS

The biggest difference between scanners and digital cameras is the way in which resolution applies to the image file. Scanners offer many variations on resolution; the higher the resolution, the larger the file size. With digital cameras, resolution is defined not by the number of pixels per inch but by the number of pixels the CCD can capture in total. This limitation controls the ultimate file size and amount of information it can hold. That is why, when looking at digital camera specifications, you see information about file size and pixel dimension but not resolution.

Today's market includes several high-output digital cameras that might be the solution to your digitizing needs if your project includes objects too large for a flatbed scanner. These cameras are called *scanbacks*. They actually function as miniscanners attached to large-format cameras like 4 × 5 view cameras. The scanback moves a CCD along the length of the capture area to create the digital file, in effect acting much like a CCD in a flatbed scanner. Scanbacks are the only digital cameras that can capture at high enough resolutions to meet most digital project benchmarks. The one drawback to these cameras is the cost, upward of $25,000. Although hundreds of digital cameras are on the market, the files sizes most of them produce are too small for anything other than web page use and small hard copy prints.

Figures 6.1 through 6.4 are examples of digital image files generated using a Phase One FX digital scanback camera, mounted on a Toyo 4 × 5 view camera. As you can see, the use of a digital camera allows for the capture of a variety of collection material, including a baseball autographed by Hall-of-Famer Grover Cleveland Alexander, who played on the 1928 World Series St. Louis Cardinals team (the Cardinals lost to the New York Yankees in three straight games) and a bound volume featuring advertisements for the Metz Brothers Brewery in Omaha, Nebraska. The binding on this volume is too tight to invert for scanning on a flatbed scanner, so it was supported with pads and digitized from above. Furniture can be digitized using digital cameras. Figure 6.3 is a desk that measures approximately thirty inches high, and figure 6.4 is a banner from the Crete, Nebraska, Prohibition Club that measures approximately twenty-four inches across. Utilizing the Phase One FX enabled digital capture at

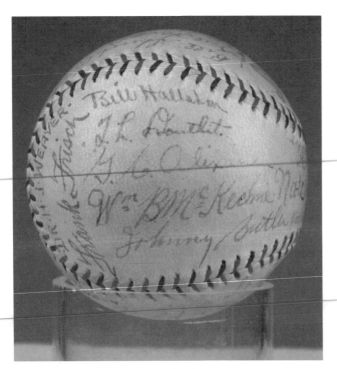

Figure 6.1 NSHS Museum Collections 9646-4.

high resolutions to produce image files not just for website use but for possible publication if necessary. Note the color bar used in each image except the autographed baseball.[5] This tool helps users determine accurate color representation for viewing and printing purposes.[6]

Finally, when considering the purchase of a digital camera, remember this: The reason to buy a digital camera is because the object you want to digitize is too large for your flatbed scanner. As an example, let's say you want to digitize a map like the one in figure 6.5. The map has a lot of detailed information that researchers want to access on your website. When you photograph the map with a digital camera, you, in essence, shrink the map to a very small size. When you open the digital file, you are expanding back to the size of the map. Problems may result, however, if you do not have enough pixels to enlarge the file for researchers to see the detailed information. You start large, you shrink to a CCD's pixel dimensions, and you expand,

Figure 6.2 NSHS Museum Collections 5833-15.

Figure 6.3   NSHS Museum Collections 6180-2.

but you can never quite get back to the original detail. High-end digital cameras, like the Phase One FX scanback, can capture enough information in the image file to allow researchers to see the small detail in the map, as in figure 6.6. Most digital cameras, however, will not capture enough information. Figure 6.7 is an image file created using a point and shoot digital camera of the same map digitized using the Phase One FX. Figure 6.7, which shows the whole map, does not look that different from figure 6.5. Note the lack of detail, however, in the close-up of the map, figure 6.8. This is a direct result of not having enough pixels recorded in the initial image capture. Inexpensive digital cameras will create nice digital images but will not provide detail.

If your institution cannot afford to purchase a high-end digital camera, consider finding an outsourcing company to digitize your large objects or work on collection materials that do not require such specialized equipment.

Figure 6.4   NSHS Museum Collections 3578-1.

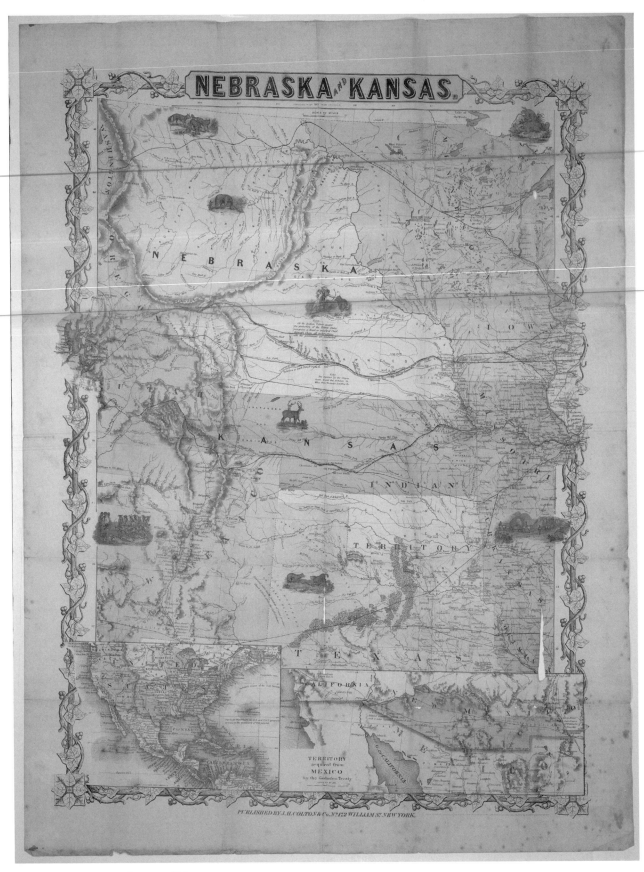

Figure 6.5   NSHS Forke Map #29.

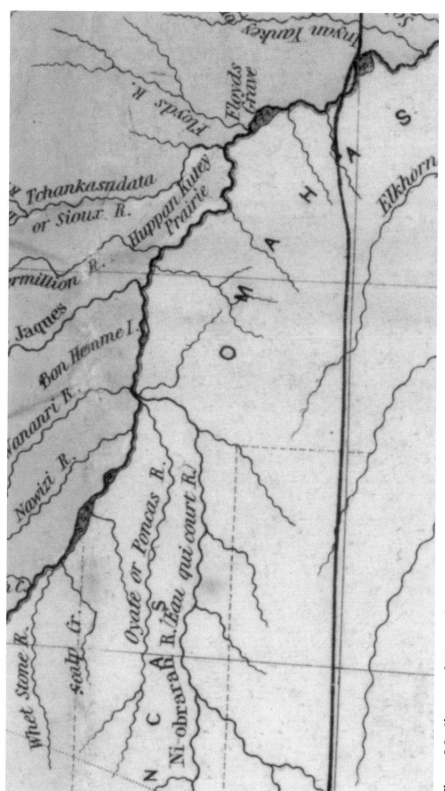

Figure 6.6   Close-up of NSHS Forke Map #29.

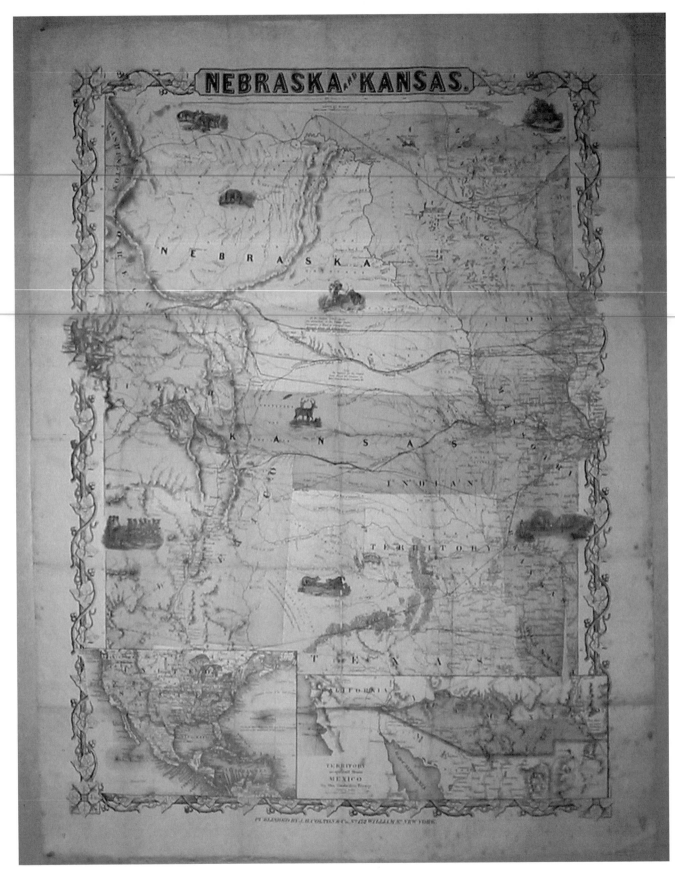

Figure 6.7   NSHS Forke Map #29.

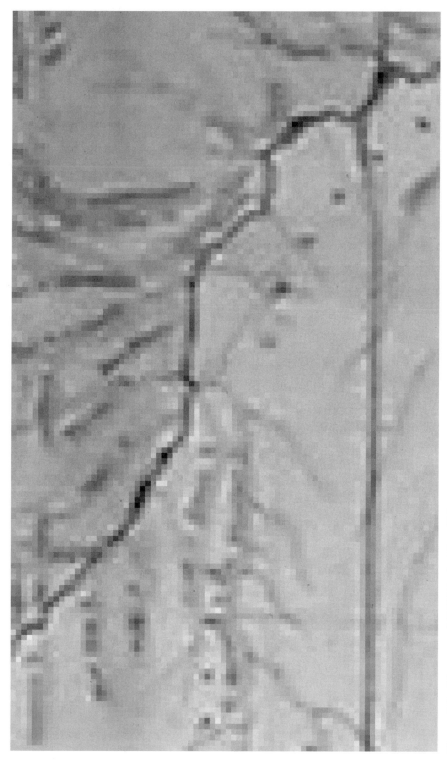

Figure 6.8   Close-up of NSHS Forke Map #29.

Another solution for digitizing oversize objects is to scan photographic reproductions of those objects. Create sharp 4 × 5 transparencies (see figure 6.9) of the oversize objects to be digitized, and then scan the film at a high resolution on your flatbed scanner. If the quality of your photographic copy if good, the results will be, too (see figure 6.10).

CONCLUSION

Buying digital imaging equipment can seem overwhelming. Make things easier by talking to your colleagues at other institutions who are already involved in digital imaging projects. Find out what kind of equipment they use and what they like and dislike about it. Ask them about software controls, dynamic range, and optical resolution.

In the end, it always comes down to money. Buy the best equipment you can afford, but be realistic. There are good scanners on the market that won't break the bank but will allow you to meet your benchmarks. Pay attention to the software controls and match the scanner specifications to your benchmarks, and you will be in good shape to conduct a digital project.

NOTES

1. Return to chapter 5 to get information on file formats and size recommendations.
2. See chapter 5 for information on file formats and size recommendations.
3. See chapter 5's section on "How to Achieve Image Files That Pass Quality Control."
4. The CCD is the capture mechanism on a scanner; see chapter 1, "A Digital Glossary."
5. No color bar was used with the baseball, because color was determined not to be a significant factor with this object.
6. See chapter 5's discussion of "Dealing with Color."

Figure 6.9   NSHS Museum Collection 9349-1.

Figure 6.10   Close-up of NSHS
Museum Collection 9349-1.

CHAPTER 7

How to Track Digital Image Files: Metadata and Databases

THE TERM *METADATA* LITERALLY MEANS DATA ABOUT data. Data is information. Digital image files are data. Tracking data about data may seem confusing, but it is really just the act of recording information about an item. Metadata about digital image files is simply information about those files organized within a framework of data elements. Think of an element as a field in a database. It can include only one type of information. For example, a date element can include only a date; it cannot include subject information, such as the names of people mentioned in the digitized letter. Metadata can consist of a multitude of information—everything from specific characteristics of the image file, through information about the creation of the file, to information about the content of the image file. Metadata can also include information about the original object used to generate the digital image file. What type of metadata you capture and how detailed that metadata is will impact the longevity of your image files and how those files are retrieved by researchers on the Internet.

METADATA STANDARDS

The most important thing about metadata is that it be recorded in a standardized way, with standards not only for what elements are used but also for the way the data is entered within those elements. This is cataloging, with the difference that the catalog record is about the digital image file rather than the original object, although some digital projects are incorporating elements to describe the original as well.[1]

The need for standards in metadata is not new. Libraries, archives, and museums have utilized cataloging for many years to provide access to their collections. Those catalog records are just like metadata records, except they describe original objects rather than digital versions. The Dublin Core element set is rapidly becoming the standard for describing digital objects.[2] Dublin Core is the name for a set of fifteen elements designed to create a set of metadata that can be used by any institution to describe digital objects mounted on the Internet. If multiple institutions describe their metadata using the same elements, their data is compatible and can be combined for searching by researchers.

A good example of the benefits of multi-institution use of Dublin Core is the Colorado Digitization Project (CDP; www.cdpheritage.org/). The CDP, funded by the Institute for Museum and Library Services, began as a project designed to create digital archives of collection materials from libraries, archives, and museums across the state of Colorado. Each institution created digital files of selected collections and then used the Dublin Core data elements to describe their digital files. Because everyone used the Dublin Core elements, regardless of the size of the institution or the type of collection, cross-institution collection searching is possible. The CDP added a few elements to the standard Dublin Core set. This was done with the consensus of the participating institutions because they wanted to create separate elements for the dates of the original object versus the date the digital version was generated. This same idea was used to create elements to help researchers distinguish between the format of the digital version and the format of the original object. An element for the name of the holding institution was also added to identify where the original object is located. (The Dublin Core Metadata Initiative does not recognize these additions, but the CDP and their project participants find them useful.) The CDP has now expanded its collaborative digitization project beyond the borders of Colorado and is creating multiple state, multiple institution projects utilizing Dublin Core metadata.

Note: Most funders do not require digital imaging projects to use Dublin Core metadata elements, but you should seriously consider this option as it will make your data compatible with other nationally recognized projects. This will make your institution and your digital projects potential partners for future online collaborative efforts. *Collaboration* is the buzzword for digital imaging funders.

Dublin Core Element Set[3]
Title
Creator
Subject
Description
Publisher
Contributor
Date
Type
Format
Identifier
Source
Language
Relation
Coverage
Rights

CDP Element Set[4]
Title
Creator
Subject
Description
Publisher
Contributor
Date.Original
Date.Digital
Resource type
Format.Use
Format.Creation
Resource identifier
Source
Language
Relation
Coverage
Rights
Holding.Institution

METADATA AND THE CREATION OF IMAGE FILES

To help authenticate your image files, you need to track data about the creation of the files. Here is a chart showing metadata elements that describe the creation and original source of a digital image file (see table 7.1). These are not Dublin Core elements, but the data de-

scribed will fit within the Dublin Core element set. These elements include information about the object number; the format of the original (e.g., is it a letter, a postcard, or a quilt); the size of the original; and a brief description. The elements used for describing the digital image file include file name; file type (e.g., the master file, the print file, the reference file, or the thumbnail); the file location; file format; resolution; color information (grayscale or RGB); capture equipment record of what scanner was used to create the file (important because as you continue to digitize, your equipment will change); capture date (the day the file was created, to help you determine which file is the master if you run into trouble with authenticating files); the name of the person who created the file; and the date on which the file should first be checked for refreshment.(Note: It is possible to include all of the information about the digital file listed above within the Dublin Core element Format or the CDP element Format.Creation.)

Table 7.1 Metadata Elements of a Digital Image File

Metadata—Creation of Digital Image File	
Original Source	*Digital File*
Item Number	File Name
Format	File Type
Size	File Location
Description	File Format
	Resolution
	Grayscale or RGB
	Capture Equipment
	Capture Date
	Name of Scanning Technician
	Begin Date for Refreshment

Not all metadata needs to be available for researchers, so you may decide not to incorporate all of the file creation metadata into your online metadata catalog. You will notice there is no information about the name of the scanning technician in most online catalog records describing digital objects. All of the metadata is important to capture, but not all of it is necessary for researchers.

DATA ENTRY METHODS

Establishing a standard set of metadata elements is only the first step in creating accurate metadata. Once you are ready to actually record data, you must use a standardized tool or language within the data. For example, under the subject element, use a thesaurus when describing

Figure 7.1 NSHS RG5251.PH-30.

the content of the image file. This is particularly important when more than one person is entering data. However, using a standard descriptive language will also help researchers searching your data. For example, here is a list of possible subjects for the photograph shown in figure 7.1: house, windmill, cornfield, barn.

All four terms seem like logical words to enter in the subject element. Let's compare these terms with the terms listed in the Library of Congress Subject Headings (LCSH) available online at http://authorities.loc.gov/. *House* is an accepted LCSH. *Windmill* is not; the correct term is *windmills*, plural. *Cornfield* is not an accepted subject heading, so you might instead use the more general term *agriculture* or just the word *corn*. Like *windmill*, *barn* is also listed in the plural form, *barns*, in the LCSH.

Another thesaurus now available online is the thesaurus for graphic materials (TGM), available at www.loc.gov/rr/print/tgm1/. The TGM is often much simpler to use than the LCSH. After searching for your term, the results include broader terms, narrower terms, and related terms all on the same page. This makes for much faster results and ease of use, although the TGM is not nearly as complete in terms of sheer numbers of entries as the LCSH. For example, entering a search for *barn* in the TGM results in the accepted term *barns* as well as the broader term *agricultural facilities* and the related term *stables*. Narrower terms and related terms often help a cataloger better describe the item. One in-

teresting term that does not appear in the TGM, although it is an accepted LC subject heading, is *house*. The TGM uses the term *dwellings* or *houses*. With any thesaurus, it is important to be creative in searching.

You will also see terms in thesauri that are geographically divisible. This means when you use the term, you must also include the country or state and city if it is known. *Barns*, *corn*, *houses*, and *windmills* are all geographically divisible. When used in metadata, they should be entered as *Barns--Nebraska*. In this case, we do not know where in Kimball County the image was taken, so there is no city to include. If we did know the city, the entry would look like this: *Barns--Nebraska--Bushnell*.

It is very important to use a thesaurus when entering subject information. This will help make your data compatible with other online resources as well as making the search easier for researchers. Be sure to include on your website which thesaurus or thesauri you used for data entry as an additional help to the researcher.

BUILDING A DATABASE FOR METADATA

Database construction is highly dependent on which database program you use. The important thing to remember is to make a separate field for each type of data or element you want to record. What follows is a brief description of how to create a metadata database in MS Access that includes the CDP's metadata element set as well as additional fields to describe in more detail the creation of the digital file.

First, create a new database and give it a name. Consider using a name not specific to your project, as you will probably continue to scan your collection once your initial project is complete. Within the database, create a table that consists of fields for each of the CDP's elements listed in table 7.2: title, creator, subject, and so forth.

Table 7.2 Metadata Database CDP's Elements Table

Field Name	Field Length	Required (yes/no)
Title	255 characters	yes
Creator	255	yes, if available
Subject	255 or memo	yes
Description	memo	yes
Publisher	255	no
Contributor	255	no
Date.Original	25	yes, if applicable
Date.Digital	25	yes
Resource Type	255	no
Format.Use	255	yes
Format.Creation	255	yes
Resource Identifier	255	yes
Source	255	no
Language	100	no, but recommended if applicable
Relation	255	no
Coverage	255	no, but recommended for maps
Rights	255	yes, if available
Holding.Institution	255	yes

For a complete listing and full description information about each of the CDP's elements, please refer to *Western States Dublin Core Element Set, Version 1.1*, November 2002, available online at www.cdpheritage .org/resource/metadata/index.html. The material used in this chapter to describe the CDP element set comes directly from this document and is used with permission of the CDP.

Once your table is complete, create a form based on the table to make data entry easier for your staff. Data can be entered directly into the table, but using a form often lessens eye strain and makes data entry go more quickly. Many database programs will allow you to import an image file directly into the database. This is a terrific advantage because it visually links your data to the image file and mistakes are easily discovered. Once your database is built and you have begun data entry, talk with the people who will be constructing your web-

site about integrating your data and image files online. If you are building your own website, you will need to talk to your host provider about space issues and support for your database and image files.

Figure 7.2 shows the main entry screen for the Digital Image Metadata databases used by the Nebraska State Historical Society. This database tracks all of the information about the creation of the image file, the original source information, and the refreshment cycle data. The data is searchable by scan file name, CD location, or original object number. There are two main tables in this database, one called DIL-L, which stands for digital imaging lab–Lincoln, and the other, DIL-O, which stands for digital imaging lab–Omaha. Data from these two labs are kept separate because the two facilities do not share the same server. Figure 7.3 shows the main data entry form for assigning a new scan file name to a digital image file. On the left is the information about the original object. This information is designed specifically for the various collecting divisions of the Nebraska State Historical Society. The information on the right relates to the creation of the digital image file and includes scheduling for refreshment.

CONCLUSION

It may take your staff some time and effort to learn database design and construction, but the database programs available today offer tremendous flexibility with a short learning curve. The key to good database design is knowing exactly the data you want to record and how you want to retrieve it before you start creating the database.

NOTES

1. See the Colorado Digitization Project Metadata element set, available online at www.cdpheritage.org/ westerntrails/wt_bpmetadata.html.
2. For more information about Dublin Core, see the Dublin Core Metadata Initiative website at http:// dublincore.org.
3. For a detailed description of each Dublin Core element, go to http://dublincore.org/documents/dces/.
4. For a detailed description of the CDP Dublin Core element set, see *Western State Dublin Core Metadata Element Set Version 1.1*, November 2002, available online at www.cdpheritage.org/resource/metadata/ index.html.

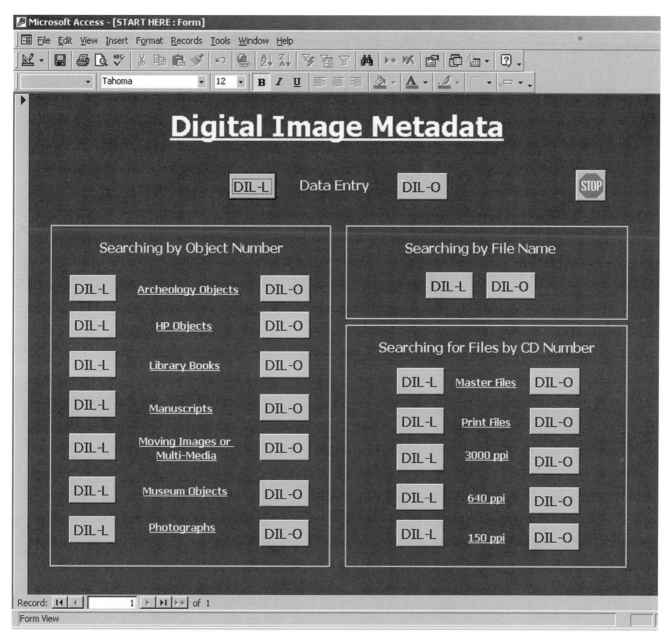

Figure 7.2 NSHS Digital Image Metadata Database.

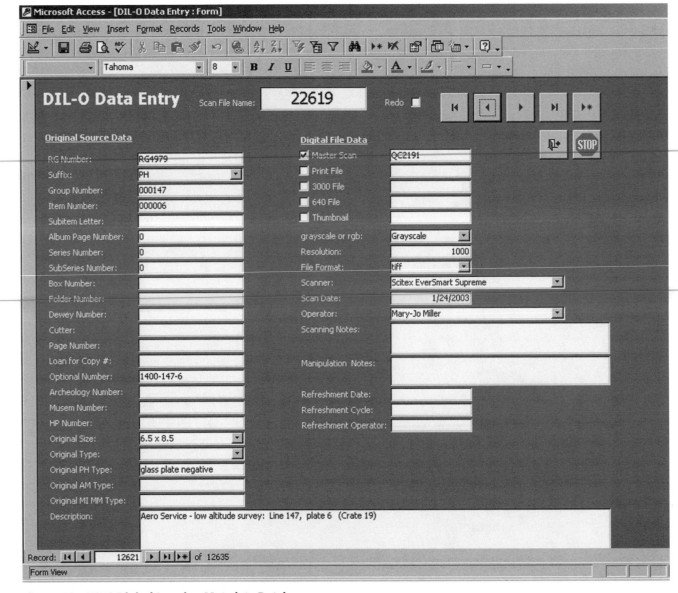

Figure 7.3 NSHS Digital Imaging Metadata Database.

CHAPTER 8

Revealing History:
Image Enhancement as a Research Tool

ALTHOUGH DIGITAL IMAGING IS NOW WELL INGRAINED in our culture—most television commercials, advertisements, and news photography are all digital—we often ignore the benefits of this technology without even realizing it. One aspect of this technology in particular is frequently overlooked, not only by the creators of digital image files but also by the researchers who use those files. Most institutions that embark on digital imaging projects do so in order to give researchers, regardless of where they live, access to the plethora of wonderful materials in their collections. Additionally, they want to protect their collections from wear due to extensive handling.

That was exactly the goal of the Nebraska State Historical Society (NSHS) when staff began generating digital image files in 1998. The initial project, funded by Ameritech and the Library of Congress National Digital Library Award Program, produced in electronic form roughly two-thirds of the Solomon D. Butcher photograph collection and approximately three hundred letters dating from 1862 to 1911 in the Uriah Oblinger family collection. Altogether approximately nine thousand digital image files were created over two years.

Solomon Butcher was a photographer working in central Nebraska, an area commonly known as the Sandhills. Butcher's intent was to document the end of the homesteading era. His photographs of sod houses and the determined people who built them are familiar to any American who has seen documentary films on the West, read books about European settlement in the Great Plains, or taken an American history class. The Oblinger letters made up the second half of the project because they offer important testimony about the life of homesteaders on the Great Plains. Together these two collections give a real sense of what life was like for homesteaders struggling to "prove-up" in the Sandhills of Nebraska. The collections are available online as part of the American Memory portion of the Library of

Congress website and can be found at http://memory .loc.gov/ammem/award98/nbhihtml/pshome.html.

Starting the first major digital imaging project with these two premier collections was an obvious choice for the NSHS. For over fifty years, the Butcher photographs have served as the illustration of homesteading on the Great Plains. Numerous books, articles, and documentary films have utilized these engaging images. Society staff thought they knew everything there was to know about the photographs. They were wrong.

As the staff began scanning the plates, it immediately became apparent that there was more information in the photographs than initially realized. By the very nature of photography, negatives always hold more detail than prints. The negative is the first thing to be exposed, thus creating the photograph. The print is simply a mechanism to make the image more easily viewed. A black-and-white photographic print contains many shades of gray, from the deepest black in shadow areas to the whitest white in the highlights of the image. In a traditional darkroom, a printer must "pull in" the highlights, by printing them darker in order to maintain detail. The opposite is true for shadow areas. The printer must "hold" the shadows and make sure they do not get too dark, thus losing detail. A good black-and-white print shows black shadow areas and white highlights with detail. This information is only apparent, however, when captured in the original negative.

The advances made in the last several years in scanning technology have allowed for capturing increasingly higher resolution and longer density ranges. This translates into pulling more information from the original object during the scanning process than ever before. More information in the electronic file leads to better understanding of the original.

In July 1998, when the NSHS began scanning the Butcher negatives, the depth of information "hidden" in the plates that never appeared in the prints immedi-

Figure 8.1 Unidentified Family Northwest of West Union, Nebraska, 1886. Solomon D. Butcher Collection, Nebraska State Historical Society RG2608.PH-1100.

Figure 8.2 Close-up of NSHS RG2608.PH-1100.

ately became apparent. Until digitization began, researchers were required to use microfiche, generated in the late 1980s, to look at the collection. If the fiche was not adequate for their needs, they were allowed to use copy prints and sometimes original prints made from the glass plates. No one ever thought about looking at the negatives, because the prints were available. And those prints are loaded with good information about homesteading. The question never came up to suggest that there might be more to the images than met the eye—until the NSHS staff started scanning.

Figures 8.1 through 8.10 represent some of the more poignant examples of that hidden information and how staff at the NSHS revealed the rest of the history documented so well by Butcher over one hundred years ago. In each photograph is a digital close-up that shows detail hidden in the earlier print. The faces may be familiar but the details not. Remember, as you look at these photographs, the information in those dark doorways had not been seen since Butcher released the shutter, exposed the negative, and first created the photograph. The implications for historical research are mind-boggling. Digital imaging allows us to offer researchers the chance to see what only Butcher had seen before.

Figure 8.3 Grocery Store in Overton, Nebraska, 1904. Solomon D. Butcher Collection, Nebraska State Historical Society RG2608.PH-2556.

Figure 8.4 Close-up of NSHS RG2608.PH-2556.

When you plan a digital project, consider the implications for historical research, and expand your ideas about what to digitize. Remember, though, that this type of "revealing history" is only possible when scanning from original in-camera negatives. If there is no information in the negative, there will be no information in the scan.

It is interesting to note that staff at the NSHS are discovering a number of people in photographs who had gone unnoticed until the images were digitized (see figures 8.8 through 8.10). This speaks to the power of digital imaging and the fact that this new technology is forcing even trained professionals to look more closely at the materials in their collections.

The same techniques used to open up the shadow details in digital images of photographic negatives can also be applied to just about any digital image regardless of the original object's format. The key is to work with a digital file generated directly from the original object. Figure 8.11 shows a sample of a handwritten letter that is quite difficult to read. A few adjustments to the contrast of the image file and the

Figure 8.5   The Laurelman Family, Northeast Custer County, Nebraska, 1886. Solomon D. Butcher Collection, Nebraska State Historical Society RG2608.PH-1062.

Figure 8.6   Close-up of NSHS RG2608.PH-1062.

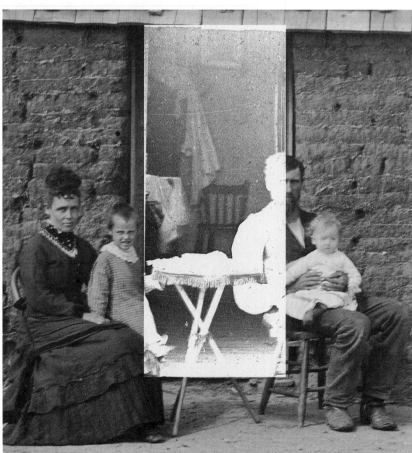

Figure 8.7   Solomon D. Butcher Collection, Nebraska State Historical Society RG2608.PH-1523.

Figure 8.8   Close-up of NSHS RG2608.PH-1523. Two children and possibly an adult were standing inside the house while the photograph was taken. Why? It is possible they were visiting neighbors and not part of the family, so they were not included in the photograph. The little boy just inside the doorway does not look very happy to be excluded from the photograph.

Figure 8.9   MacDonald Studio Collection, Nebraska State Historical Society RG2183.PH:1933-0411.

writing is much easier to read (see figure 8.12). This type of manipulation is quick and easy and gives quite dramatic results.

When working with image manipulation software to help researchers learn more about the original, be sure to include information about exactly what was done to the image file. This gets back to the issue of ethics. Although manipulation to enhance information is not like offering a file with added information that did not exist, it is important that anyone using the enhanced files know they are enhanced. It is a matter of truth and authenticity. If researchers working with enhanced digital files are unaware of the manipulation, they will be surprised at the state of the original if they get a chance to see it.

Figure 8.10   Close-up of NSHS RG2183.PH:1933-0411. This young man is peeking around a corn alcohol advertisement. Perhaps he was a shy employee who did not want his photograph taken, or perhaps he realized at the last minute that the other gentlemen in the photograph were police officers.

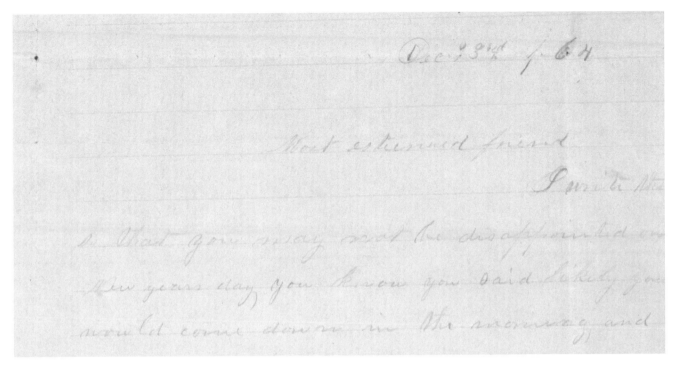

Figure 8.11   Close-up of NSHS RG1346.AM.S01.L013.

IMAGE RECOVERY FROM DETERIORATING ORIGINALS

Staff at the NSHS discovered another benefit to digitizing that had not been considered in the original project planning. A common malady found in photographic collections is negatives turned yellow due to mercuric iodide intensification. These negatives are very difficult to print in the darkroom, because the yellowed areas on the negative are virtually transparent. Modern photographic papers do not have the tonal range to detect the

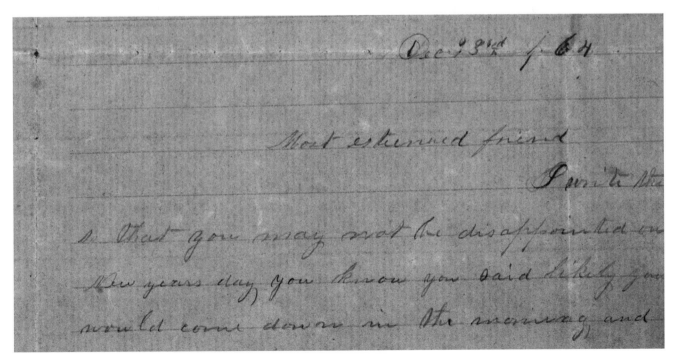

Figure 8.12   Close-up of NSHS RG1346.AM.S01.L013.

Figure 8.13   NSHS RG2608.PH-2674.

slight changes in value in the deteriorated negatives. Many institutions gave up on these negatives years ago, forgetting about them or in some cases disposing of them completely. If the information in the negative cannot be retrieved, why take up precious storage space to hold objects of no value to researchers? Digital imaging turns these once unusable negatives into viable research tools.

One of the Butcher negatives (figure 8.13) suffers from mercuric iodide intensification. On a lark, a scan

was attempted with little expectation of success. The results were amazing (see figure 8.14). The scanner was able to record the subtle differences between tonal values in the affected areas of the image, enabling the content of the glass plate negative to be viewed.

Since that first test, the NSHS staff have scanned numerous yellow negatives. No manipulation was necessary for the scanner to detect the shades of yellow. The negatives are scanned as if they were unaffected black-and-white negatives, and the scanner looks at the shifts

Figure 8.14   NSHS RG2608.PH-2674.

in tonal value and records a positive grayscale image. Slight adjustments to contrast in surrogate image files help to produce high-quality prints and reference files for use online. The master files remain untouched, as close a representation of the original as possible. Prior to scanning, these yellow negatives were virtually worthless. Now they are an important part of the collection. As scanner technology improves, the ability to pull more and more information from deteriorated originals will continue.[1]

For you to see what an original glass plate looks like, a piece of white paper was laid on top of the negative and then scanned as if it were a print. That way you can see how faint the image is due to the deterioration of the plate (see figures 8.15 through 8.18).

This is the best example to date of image recovery from a deteriorating glass plate negative (see figures 8.19 and 8.20). The original plate holds very little detail, but once digitized using a scanner with a 3.7 density range, the detail is readily apparent, making this

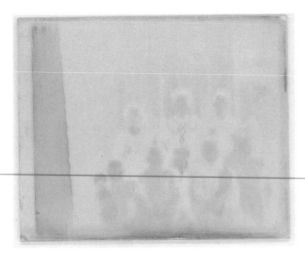

Figure 8.15   NSHS RG1722.PH:2-2.

Figure 8.16   NSHS RG1722.PH:2-2.

Figure 8.17   Close-up of NSHS RG1722.PH:2-2. This view of the previous plate shows the amazing results of digital recovery.

Figure 8.18.   Close-up of NSHS RG1722.PH:2-2.

Figure 8.19   NSHS RG1722.PH:5-38.

Figure 8.20   NSHS RG1722.PH:5-38.

photograph useful for researchers. Digital imaging is an amazing tool that offers historical institutions of all sizes the ability to expand the use of their collections in a safe and productive way while at the same time learning more about their objects than ever before.

NOTE

1. The material in this chapter was published in a previous form in *Nebraska History* 81, no. 2 (Summer 2000): 50–55, and *Spectra* 26, no. 2 (Fall 2000): 10–15.

Suggested Readings

COPYRIGHT ISSUES

Besek, June M. *Copyright Issues Relevant to the Creation of a Digital Archive: A Preliminary Assessment.* Commissioned for and sponsored by the National Digital Information Infrastructure and Preservation Program. Washington, D.C.: Library of Congress, Council on Library and Information Resources, January 2003.[1]

Harris, Lesley Ellen. *Licensing Digital Content: A Practical Guide for Librarians.* Chicago: American Library Association, 2002.

Shapiro, Michael S., and Brett I. Miller. *A Museum Guide to Copyright and Trademark.* Washington, D.C.: American Association of Museums, 1999.

DIGITAL IMAGING

Hunter, Gregory S. *Preserving Digital Information: A How-To-Do-It Manual for Librarians.* Number 93. New York: Neal-Schuman, 2000.

Kenney, Anne R., and Oya Y. Rieger. *Moving Theory into Practice: Digital Imaging for Libraries and Archives.* Mountain View, Calif.: Research Libraries Group, 2000.

Sitts, Maxine K., ed. *Handbook for Digital Projects: A Management Tool for Preservation and Access.* Andover, Mass.: Northeast Document Conservation Center, 2000.

METADATA

Baca, Murtha. *Introduction to Metadata: Pathways to Digital Information.* N.p.: Getty Information Institute, The J. Paul Getty Trust, 1998.

ONLINE RESOURCES

American Institute for Conservation of Historic and Artistic Works: http://aic.stanford.edu/

American Memory, Building Digital Collections: Technical Information and Background Papers: http://memory.loc.gov/ammem/ftpfiles.html

Besser, Howard, and Jennifer Trant. *Introduction to Imaging: Issues in Constructing an Image Database*: www.getty.edu/research/institute/standards/introimages/

Colorado Digitization Program: www.cdpheritage.org/

Conservation OnLine: http://palimpsest.stanford.edu/

Council on Library and Information Resources: www.clir.org

Digital Library Federation: www.diglib.org/

Dublin Core Metadata Initiative: http://dublincore.org/

Museum Computer Network: www.mcn.edu/resources/index.htm

Grant Funding Resources

National Historical Publications and Records Commission: www.archives.gov/grants/index.html

National Endowment for the Arts: www.nea.gov

National Endowment for the Humanities: www.neh.gov

Subject Indexing

Library of Congress Subject Headings: http://authorities.loc.gov/webvoy.htm

Thesaurus for Graphic Materials: www.loc.gov/rr/print/tgm1/

NOTE

1. It is worth looking at any CLIR publication associated with digital imaging. The Council on Library and Information Resources will always have the newest information on any issue that might affect digital projects.

Index

Jill Marie Koelling spent seven and a half years working for the Nebraska State Historical Society as curator of photographs and head of digital imaging. During that time, she developed two state-of-the-art digital imaging laboratories and successfully transitioned the institution from analog production to the digital arena. Koelling is now applying her digital imaging expertise in the Special Collections and Archives at Cline Library, Northern Arizona University, where the goal is to create an online archive featuring a majority of the collection. Along with her interest in the impact digital imaging has on historical collections, Koelling is writing a book featuring the early auto-touring exploits of Edward and Margaret Gehrke.